What better way to spend a sunny Sunday afternoon, than to have a trip out from Newport docks on the splendid steam tug *Dunhawk*. It is 18 June 1967 and it would appear that wives and girlfriends have joined the crew of the tug as she sets out on another job in the twilight of her towing career. The *Dunhawk* was completed in 1943 by Henry Scarr at Hessle as the *Empire Maisie*, a Birch-class Empire tug for the Ministry of War Transport. She was powered by a triple-expansion steam engine with an output of 1000ihp. In 1947 she passed to Clyde Shipping Co Ltd as *Flying Typhoon* and was based on the River Clyde. She arrived at Newport in 1960 when she was purchased by Newport Screw Towing Co Ltd and named *Dunhawk*. In 1968 she was replaced by a motor tug and was sold to John Cashmore who broke her up locally on the River Usk.

(the late John Wiltshire)

1

This is an interesting elevated view of Newport Screw Towing's tug berth in a corner of the North Dock at Newport, taken on 14 April 1968. The two steam tugs **Dunfalcon** and **Dunhawk** dominate the picture, while the bow of the motor tug **Duncurlew** is just visible on the right. Her sistership **Dunsnipe** lies ahead of the steam tugs, while in the distance is the recently delivered motor tug **Dunosprey**. Also of note in this view is a pair of locally-built motor trawlers moored on the buoys in the middle of the dock. These were built for the Ghana Fishing Corporation which was initially unable to complete payment for the vessels when built. Newport's famous transporter bridge dating from 1906 can also be seen in the background.

(the late John Wiltshire)

In 1960 the British Transport Commission took delivery of a pair of twin-screw motor tugs for use at Newport docks. They were built in North Devon by P K Harris and Sons Ltd at Appledore and were given local Newport place names. The first to arrive was **St. Woolos** in January followed by **Llanwern** in June. This view was taken in the fading afternoon sun of 24 February 1968. It shows **St. Woolos** and **Llanwern** waiting at the entrance to the main lock. Once the lock had flooded and the gates were open, the Newport Screw Towing tugs would leave the lock and head back to their berth. The two dock tugs would then move into the lock and take over the berthing of the vessel. Quite a protracted affair, but nonetheless a fascinating one.

(the late John Wiltshire)

Newport Screw Towing Company Limited took delivery of their first motor tugs during 1962, the *Duncurlew* and *Dunsnipe*. At the time, with a bhp of 1260, these were the most powerful tugs in South Wales. The *Duncurlew* was delivered from her builder Richard Dunston (Hessle) Ltd, Hessle, Humberside in September 1962 and would have replaced at least one steam tug. In this view taken in the late afternoon of 12 July 1969, the *Duncurlew* is seen in the South Dock having left the lock, and is approaching the narrow passage into the North Dock. A few minutes earlier she would have used her horn to signal for the swing bridge over the passage to be opened, enabling all the returning tugs to reach their berth.

(the late John Wiltshire)

By the time I began to visit Newport docks in early 1967 the *Dunfalcon* was the spare tug. I got used to seeing the *Dunhawk* together with the motor tugs *Duncurlew* and *Dunsnipe* in action, and so I was pleased to witness the *Dunfalcon* in action on at least two occasions. The *Dunfalcon* dated from 1941 and was completed on the Clyde as *Empire Pine* by Scott and Sons, Bowling, for the Ministry of War Transport. She was one of the first Empire tugs completed, being an example of the *Warrior* class, and was sold to Steel and Bennie Ltd, Glasgow in 1946. They renamed her *Vanguard* and later *Battleaxe*, before selling her to Newport Screw Towing Co Ltd in 1961. Here she is on a gloomy day in February 1966. The *Dunfalcon* was broken up in early 1969 alongside *Dunhawk* on the banks of the River Usk at Newport.

(Danny Lynch)

The motor tug *Newport* was the smallest of the three dock tugs based at Newport when this photograph was taken on 21 March 1971. She was completed by W J Yarwood and Sons of Northwich for the British Transport Commission. She was powered by a British Polar diesel of 700bhp driving a single screw. When *Newport* entered service in 1956, she would be working alongside the steam tugs *Trusty* of 1913 and *Gwent* of 1949. Their main duties were ship-handling within the confines of Newport docks. From 1963 her owner became the British Transport Docks Board (BTDB), by which time the steam tugs had been sold. From 1967 her funnel colour changed to that illustrated here, and by 1970 her hull changed from black to beige. By the 1970s *Newport* saw considerably less use, only being called upon when a dock move required three tugs, or one of the twin-screw motor tugs was out of action. She was laid up by 1977 and was sold by the BTDB to Egyptian owners in 1978. There has been no further information as to her ultimate fate or even if she ever made it to her initial reported destination of Port Said.

(Danny Lynch)

The **Dunsnipe** was delivered to Newport Screw Towing in December 1962. She was an attractive looking tug of 186 gross tons with an overall length of just under 101 feet. However she was quite primitive for her time, as she did not feature bridge-control of the main engine. The engine was a 2-stroke British Polar and the transmission did not include a reverse gear. To go astern the engine would have to be stopped, and then reversed, which caused a delay. In this view taken on 18 April 1970, the **Dunsnipe** is heading out from the lock to meet an incoming ship. In the background we can see some of the pylons that lead from Uskmouth Power station. Later that year Newport Screw Towing sold out to R & J H Rea Ltd. Rea passed to Cory Ship Towage Ltd in 1971 and the **Dunsnipe** was renamed **Gwentgarth**.

(the late John Wiltshire)

The **Dunosprey** was in many ways a development of the earlier motor tugs **Duncurlew** and **Dunsnipe**. She came from the same shipyard at Hessle on Humberside, and was fitted with the same British Polar 2-stroke diesel engine of 1260bhp. The **Dunosprey** did however have bridge control of her main engine, and also featured a steerable kort nozzle around her propeller. Her wheelhouse was of an improved design which allowed better all-round visibility. After passing to Cory Ship Towage ownership in 1970, her time at Newport was cut short as she too was transferred to the Belfast fleet. She remained there until 1992, and for some reason was never renamed. Her port of registry had changed to Belfast by 1976. In this view a good comparison can be made with her older sisters on pages 4 and 6.

(Danny Lynch)

To replace the steam tugs **Dunfalcon** and **Dunhawk** in 1968, Newport Screw Towing purchased a new motor the **Dunosprey**, but was not in a position to obtain a second new tug. In 1968 there were very few ship-handling motor tugs for sale in the UK, as many fleets were still in the process of selling off their uneconomical steam tugs. Fortunately Tees Towing Co Ltd (Wm Crosthwaite & Son) of Middlesbrough had two for sale; and one of these, **Golden Cross**, was purchased. The **Golden Cross** had been new in 1955, and was one of three similar vessels for that fleet. Upon arrival at Newport in August 1968, **Golden Cross** gained the funnel colours of her new owner. Her hull on the other hand was in desperate need of a repaint, as can be determined in this view of her taken on 17 August 1968, shortly after arrival from the Tees. She was later given the name **Dunheron**, and took up her role as the fourth or spare tug, once the steam tugs had departed for scrap.

(the late John Wiltshire)

It is 3 April 1972 and **Llanwern** is seen pushing up to the Italian-flagged bulk carrier **Polinnia**. The tug is now carrying the final version of the British Transport Docks Board livery with a beige hull. The **Llanwern** differed from her sister **St. Woolos** as her pair of Lister Blackstone diesels powered a diesel-electric type transmission, with two electric motors driving her propeller shafts. This method was quite unusual in British tugs, and produced quite a distinctive whining sound from the engine room during manoeuvring. After at least one failed attempt, in 1977 the BTDB was able to sell off their towage operation at Newport to Cory Ship Towage. The deal included only **Llanwern** and **St. Woolos**, which were renamed **Taffgarth** and **Wyegarth** respectively. The **Taffgarth** went on bareboat charter to the port authority at Londonderry in 1979, and was eventually purchased by them and renamed **Foyledale** in 1980. By 1995 she was working for McKenzie Marine UK Ltd as **Ulla Pull** and passed to West African interests in 1999.

(the late John Wiltshire)

The **Boreas** arrived at Newport in August 1978 and had in tow a barge laden with beer vats for the new Carlsberg brewery at Magor. She was a Dutch-owned tug sailing under the Panamanian flag for Vooruitgang Is Ons Streven (H D van Vliet) of Papendrecht. The **Boreas** had been delivered in 1957 as **Fairplay VI**, a harbour tug for Fairplay Schleppdampfschiffe Reederei R Borchard of Hamburg. She was completed by Theodor Buschmann Schiffswerft at their Wilhelmsburg yard in Hamburg and had an overall length of 91 feet. Power was provided by a 7-cylinder MAN diesel of 950bhp which drove a controllable-pitch propeller. She was sold by Fairplay to her Dutch owner a couple of months prior to this photograph, and in 1979 she was renamed **Boreas 1**. Her second lease of life was to be brief as in 1980 she was laid up at Rotterdam, and by 1982 had lost her main engine upon passing to Polderman Sleepdienst & Berging of Hansweert. In 1983 she passed to the local fire service at Vlissingen as a training vessel and was substantially rebuilt. Her ultimate fate is unknown.

(Danny Lynch)

With the departure of **Dunheron** and **Dunosprey** to Belfast in 1970, the Cory Ship Towage fleet at Newport comprised **Duncurlew** and **Dunsnipe**. These tugs spent a period based at Cardiff in 1970, when Newport docks were closed for lock repairs, and the tugs were eventually renamed **Westgarth** and **Gwentgarth** respectively. In this view of **Westgarth** we are back at Newport on 21 August 1976. The tug is wearing Cory's livery which is not as distinctive as that of her previous owner Newport Screw Towing. Her stern has just been repainted and the name **Westgarth** re-applied in a rather crude fashion. From 1971

until 1977 tugs were sent from Cardiff to help out at Newport and on occasions one of the BTDB dock tugs could also be utilised for a complete towing job. The **Westgarth** was sold in 1981 to Norwegian owners at Lødingen as **Nordbever**. She was eventually re-engined and fitted with a new wheelhouse and funnel. In 2006 she became **Nico** and in 2008 **Geitung**, still under Norwegian registry. She carried the name **JK 1** from 2015, but has subsequently been recycled.

(the late John Wiltshire)

9

The tug scene at Newport went through some fairly major and rapid changes in the late 1970s and early 1980s. Consequently a number of vessels were drafted in from other parts of the Cory Ship Towage group. The **Dalegarth** of 1960 was one of four tugs built in 1959/60 to handle tankers at the newly-opened oil terminals at Milford Haven. She was built by Henry Scarr at Hessle and she was a large single-screw tug of 306 tons gross, with an overall length of 128 feet. This made her ideal for estuary work at Milford Haven, but not really that suitable for dock work. After a spell working in Canada, she moved to Avonmouth in 1978 and over to Newport in 1979. This view of **Dalegarth** taken on 12 September 1982 gives us a superb view of her ample accommodation and spacious wheelhouse. The **Dalegarth** served Newport until 1984, when she was sold to Falmouth Towage Co Ltd and renamed **St Piran**. Sold by Falmouth Towage in 2007, she had a troubled five years, mostly as a detained vessel, until she was broken up at Ghent in 2012.

(Bernard McCall)

The **Cultra** arrived at Newport in 1980 from the Belfast fleet. She had been completed in 1962 by T Mitchison Ltd at Gateshead for John Cooper (Belfast) Ltd. She was a tug of 202 tons gross with a power output of 1260bhp, and fitted with a controllable-pitch propeller. This view of **Cultra** was taken in Newport's North Dock on 27 December 1980, with the transporter bridge dominating the background. We can clearly make out the unusual design of her superstructure, with a walkway around the front of her curved wheelhouse. Also noteworthy are the twin exhaust-uptakes, in place of a traditional funnel, and the use of cream paint on her lower accommodation. This was soon repainted brown in line with other South Wales tugs. The **Cultra** worked out of Newport, often being called to help out at other ports such as Cardiff. In 1983 she was replaced at Newport by a tug purchased from West Germany. The **Cultra** was sold to Frank Pearce (Tugs) Ltd, Poole, and renamed **Pullwell**, but was resold to Greek owners at Chalkis in 1985 and became **Polikos**. It is thought she was recycled in about 2016.

(the late John Wiltshire)

In this view the former BTDB tug **St. Woolos** is now sporting a black hull once again, and as **Wyegarth** is now working for Cory Ship Towage. In her new role she is no longer confined to dock work, and in this view she is out in the channel somewhere off Newport on 7 April 1980. The **Wyegarth** appears to be drifting along in a window of sunshine, bizarrely surrounded by a sea mist. Cory was keen to dispose of her, and later in the year she set sail from Newport bound for Jeddah. Her new Saudi Arabian operator had renamed her **Rana**, but the following year her name changed to **Zaretallah**. Her new owner was now given as Oriental Commercial & Shipping Co Ltd, Jeddah, and her ultimate fate is unknown.

(Danny Lynch)

The **Cashel** and her sister **Clonmel**, were single-screw fire-fighting tugs of 22 tonnes bollard pull. They were built in 1959 at the Gateshead shipyard of T Mitchison Ltd for John Cooper (Belfast) Ltd, and registered in Cork. They were based at the Whitegate oil refinery near Cork from new until 1973, when they were replaced by the larger fire-fighting tugs **Stackgarth** and **Thorngarth**, that were originally based at Milford Haven. The **Cashel** went to work at Avonmouth and was renamed **Portgarth** in 1974. She was transferred to Newport in about 1978, and this view of her was taken on 28 January 1980. She was sold to Greek owners in 1981 as **Vernicos Martha**. She later became **Aghios Nikolaos**, and was eventually broken up at Aliaga in early 2017.

(Danny Lynch)

The **Point Gilbert** has come across from the Bristol area to help out at Newport on 13 June 1983. She and her sister, **Point James**, were completed in 1972 by Richard Dunston (Hessle) Ltd, Hessle for Smit and Cory International Port Towage Ltd. They were part of a group of four tugs required for a contract at the Come-By-Chance oil refinery in Newfoundland, Canada. Upon closure of this refinery, **Point James** and **Point Gilbert** returned to the UK in 1979/80. They were based near Bristol at the recently opened Royal Portbury Dock which was in need of some larger and more powerful tugs. The **Point Gilbert** was powered by a 12-cylinder English Electric diesel which developed 2640bhp, and she was equipped for fire-fighting. In 1986 she was fitted with a retractable Aquamaster bow thruster unit which increased her bollard pull from 36 to 42 tonnes. In early 2000 Cory Towage was taken over by Wijsmuller who then sold out to Svitzer (part of the A P Møller group) and **Point Gilbert** was transferred to the Clyde fleet. She was sold in 2005 and was with Russian owners by 2007 sailing as **Gangui**.

(Danny Lynch)

In 1978/79, the Marystown Shipyard of Marystown, Newfoundland, constructed three rather ugly-looking twin-screw tugs for Norwegian owner K/S Normand Tugs A/S, Skudeneshavn. They were delivered as **Normand Rock**, **Normand Rough** and **Normand Ross** and had a gross tonnage of around 499. The second vessel completed was the **Normand Rough** in February 1979. She had an overall length of 140 feet, a beam of 37 feet and was described as an anchor-handling tug and supply vessel. She was powered by a pair of 9-cylinder Wichmann diesels developing 6000bhp and had a bollard pull of 85 tonnes. In

June 1982 **Normand Rough** was damaged by an anchor and sank, but was soon raised. The following year she was sold to International Towing Ltd, London, who repaired her and renamed her **Lorna B**. Here she is on 29 July 1988 arriving at Newport with a rig for the Second Severn Crossing Project. The **Lorna B** was later sold and suffered an accommodation fire, before sinking for a second time at Cook Inlet in Alaska during August 1989. She was not recovered.

(Danny Lynch)

In 1983 Cory Ship Towage was looking to replace the *Cultra* with a more modern tug at Newport, and purchased the West German tug *Norderney* which had operated at Emden. She was owned by Ems Schlepper AG, and had been completed for them in October 1972 by Cassens Schiffswerft und Maschinenfabrik GmbH, Emden. She was powered by a 6-cylinder MWM diesel of 1300bhp giving her a bollard pull of 22 tonnes. Upon arrival at Newport in June 1983 she was renamed *Gwentgarth*, and soon entered service, allowing *Cultra* to be sold. This superb study of her was taken on 13 May 1984, with Captain George Canning at the helm on her flying bridge. The *Gwentgarth* was sold to Spanish owners Amare Marin SL at Marin in June 1997 and was renamed *Remmar*. As she was built to operate in icy waters she was a suitable purchase in 2005 for the Northern Shipping Co which renamed her *Triton*. They put her to work at Arkhangel in northern Russia, and she is thought to be still in service in 2018.

(the late John Wiltshire)

The **Gwentgarth** soon made a favourable impression at Newport, and was a popular tug with crews. When Cory were looking to replace **Dalegarth** in 1984, they returned to Ems Schlepper AG, at Emden, and were able to negotiate the purchase of the similar tug **Juist**. The **Juist** dated from 1975 and was similar in most respects to her older sister, but did have a smaller funnel. She was more powerful though at 1750bhp, and with an increased bollard pull of 26 tonnes. Upon arrival at Newport she was renamed **Emsgarth** reflecting her German origins. Cory Ship Towage was restyled Cory Towage Ltd in 1985, and the tugs adopted a new colour scheme loosely based on that of Rea fleet in the 1960s. The **Emsgarth** had just received her new colours when noted in Newport's South Dock on 5 October 1985.

(Andrew Wiltshire)

The towage contract for the Come-By-Chance oil refinery required four tugs (see page 13). Smit & Cory International Port Towage was a partnership with L Smit's International of Rotterdam and would operate these tugs. The **Point James** and **Point Gilbert** were delivered in 1972, followed by the larger **Point Carroll** and **Point Spencer** in 1973. The **Point Spencer** was completed by Richard Dunston at Hessle with a gross tonnage of 366 and was powered by a 12-cylinder vee Ruston Paxman diesel engine of 3300bhp. When the Come-By-Chance refinery closed, **Point Spencer** was chartered to Cory Ship Towage Ltd, London, for use on coastal towage, to which she was well suited with a raised foc's'le. This view of her at Newport dates from 5 October 1985 when she was carrying the colours of Cory Towage Ltd. She was in port for attention in the dry dock. In 1992 **Point Spencer** was sold to Cory Towage Ltd and by 2000 was working on the Clyde with Wijsmuller Marine. She was sold in 2003 to Towing & Salvage Noordgat, for service under the Netherlands flag, and was renamed **Hunter**. By 2010 her registry had changed to Panama and she was still at work in 2018.

(Andrew Wiltshire)

In 1993 West Coast Towing Co (UK) Ltd set up a base at Newport with four Russian-built tugs. The quartet had been built between 1974 and 1977, and had operated under the East German flag by BBB-VEB Bagger-, Bugsier-und Bergungsreederei, Rostock, until the reunification of Germany in 1990. Initially the tugs were named **Aquarius A.**, **Pisces L.**, **Scorpio N.** and **Taurus II**, but three of them received West Coast Towing-related names in 1994. The **C. A. Davis** is seen off Newport and was previously **Scorpio N.**. She had a gross tonnage of 183, and was built by Gorokhovetskiy Sudostroitelnyy Zavod at Gorokhovets. Her power was provided by a pair of 6-cylinder Russkiy diesels developing 1200bhp. In 1995 all four tugs were deemed surplus to requirements, and all passed to South American owners. The **C. A. Davis** went to Peruvian owner Trabajos Maritimos SA, Callao, and was renamed **Tramarsa 2**.

(Danny Lynch)

The **Gribbin Head** was a sister tug to **Golden Cross** (page 7 lower), and was new to Tees Towing Co Ltd, Middlesbrough, as **Ingleby Cross**. In 1968 she was sold to Fowey Harbour Commissioners and renamed **Gribbin Head** for use at this Cornish port. In 1988 she passed to Haven Marine Services Ltd, Pembroke Dock, who replaced her Crossley engine with a 16-cylinder English Electric diesel of 1200bhp that was new in 1956. Haven Marine Services were absorbed by West Coast Towing Co Ltd in 1989 which briefly used **Gribbin Head** for contract work. Here she is seen leaving the lock at Newport on 30 July 1990, having just delivered a crane barge to the port. The **Gribbin Head** was sold to Tuskar Rock Diving Co Ltd, Wexford, in 1990 and was eventually renamed **Tuskar Rock** in 1995. The following year she passed to Spanish owners Pinturas at Huelva and was still in service in 2005. In 2011 her name had changed to **Triva II**, but her owner and nationality were unknown.

(Danny Lynch)

The twin-screw tug *Taurus II* was another of the former East German vessels purchased by West Coast Towing Co (UK) Ltd in 1993. The new tug operation provided a little competition for Cory Towage Ltd in South-East Wales, but subsequently had a bigger impact on a tug fleet further down the Bristol Channel. The *Taurus II* dates from 1977 and was built as *Arni* for BBB-VEB Bagger-, Bugsier-und Bergungsreederei, Rostock. Upon entering service at Newport with West Coast Towing, *Taurus II* was placed under the Honduran flag which is how we see her in February 1994. Later that year she was renamed *Hurricane H.* and registered at Newport. She was equipped for fire-fighting, and her solid-looking hull was built to operate in ice. In 1995 as *Hurricane H.*, she was sold to Peruvian owner Trabajos Maritimos SA, Callao, and was renamed *Tramarsa 3*. She was still at work in 2018.

(Danny Lynch)

On 20 May 1998 the **Edengarth** has come across to Newport from Avonmouth to help out. In this view we can see that she is registered in Westport in the Irish Republic, and in the background is the Newport tug **Emsgarth**. The **Edengarth** was the first of four 50 tonne bollard pull conventional single-screw tugs delivered to Cory Ship Towage Ltd at Milford Haven in 1976/77. Two were equipped for fire-fighting and the other two capable of being adapted should the need arise, the **Edengarth** being one of the latter. She was completed by Richards (Shipbuilders) Ltd at their Great Yarmouth yard and had a grt of 381. Her registered owner when new was Rea Towing Co Ltd. Her main engine was a 16-cylinder vee-type Ruston-Paxman diesel of 3520bhp. The **Edengarth** was transferred to Irish Tugs Ltd in 1990 and later moved to Liverpool. During 1993 **Edengarth** and her sister **Eskgarth** was converted to fire-fighting and transferred to the Whitegate oil refinery. In 1997 **Edengarth** moved to Avonmouth regaining UK registry in 1998. She was sold to Ocean Supply Pte Ltd in 1999 as **Eden**. By 2007 she was under the Indonesian flag as **Prawira Dua**.

(Danny Lynch)

In 1994 West Coast Towing Co (UK) Ltd replaced the four former East German tugs at Newport with four much newer Russian-built vessels, dating from 1992. They were roughly to the same design as their predecessors, but were more powerful at around 1600bhp. They were named *Capt I. B. Harvey*, *I. B. Smith*, *E. L. Preston* and *Albert K.*. The first pair were purchased from Norwegian interests while the second pair came from Russian owners, and it is thought none had seen much service. A fifth similar tug was delivered new to Swansea in 1994 and named *Alice K.*. The *Albert K.* was powered by an 8-cylinder Pervomaysk diesel and had been completed as *Imakon 2* for service at St Petersburg. Here she is seen off Newport on 25 August 1996. The *Albert K.* was retained by West Coast Towing after they sold their South Wales towage operations to Wijsmuller on 10 May 2001. However in 2003 she returned to St Petersburg as *Atoll* in the ownership of Sea Fishing Port Co Ltd. By 2018 she was thought to be no longer in existence.

(Nigel Jones)

The **Conor** was owned by West Coast Towing and was used at Swansea and Port Talbot as well as for coastal towing, a task to which she was more suited. She was a former Spanish tug that was built in 1974 by Astilleros y Varaderos de Tarragona, Tarragona. She was completed as **Poblet** for the local fleet Remolques y Navegacion based at Tarragona. She was a conventional single-screw tug powered by an 8-cylinder Deutz diesel of 3000bhp which gave her a useful bollard pull of 43 tonnes. She was also equipped for fire-fighting as well as pollution-control. In 1995 she passed to West Coast Towing (UK) Ltd and was registered at Swansea. This view of her was taken off Newport in June 1999. In 2001 **Conor** moved on and was purchased by Portland Port Ltd and named **Maiden Castle**. In 2004 she became **Massai** for Somara (UK) Ltd and was registered at Fort de France, Martinique. Now based in the Caribbean she was still in service in 2017.

(Danny Lynch)

On 2 September 2002 we see **Emsgarth** approaching the lock at Newport. She is wearing the Svitzer Marine livery, which gives her a distinct northern European appearance. She passed with the Cory fleet to Wijsmuller Marine Ltd in February 2000, and then Svitzer Marine in 2001. Her near sister **Gwentgarth** having been sold five years earlier, the **Emsgarth** was now one of a dwindling number of conventional screw-driven tugs in Svitzer UK operation. The **Emsgarth** remained based at Newport until 2005, but still provided cover at Cardiff and Barry when required. In her 21 years' service at Newport, the **Emsgarth** carried four quite different liveries. In 2005 she passed to Dragage des Ports SA (DRAPOR) for service at Casablanca as the **Iltizam**, under the Moroccan flag. She was still in service in 2018.

(Nigel Jones)

Cory Towage Ltd purchased a small number of modern second-hand Z-peller tugs from Japan in the 1990s, and the first of these was the **Avongarth**. She was completed by Kanagawa Zosen, Kobe, in 1980 as **Iwashima Maru** for Naigai Unyu K.K. at Kobe. Upon her sale to Cory, she was loaded aboard a heavy-lift ship along with a tug destined for J P Knight, and delivered to the UK arriving in February 1991. She was modified for use in UK waters, given the traditional name **Avongarth**, and put to use at Avonmouth and Portbury. With a gross tonnage of 189, the **Avongarth** was a highly manoeuvrable tug, with a bollard pull of 35 tonnes. In this view she is in Wijsmuller's livery, and has come across to Newport on 5 May 2001 to assist the local tugs. The **Avongarth** was sold in 2010 to Pacific Maritime Holdings Ltd and placed under the St Vincent and Grenadines flag as **Pacific Castor**. In 2012 she was working in West Africa as **Lady Jesse II** under Liberian registry.

(Nigel Jones)

The **Svitzer Bristol** was delivered to Avonmouth in July 2003 and was the first of four similar tugs for Svitzer Marine Ltd. Svitzer decided to place the order with Spanish shipyard Astilleros Zamakona, Viscaya for this significant fleet upgrade. The **Svitzer Bristol** was actually launched as **Bristolgarth**, but this was soon changed as Svitzer introduced their corporate naming policy. The **Svitzer Bristol** is a large tug of 366grt and is powered by a pair of 6-cylinder Niigata diesels which develop a total of 4087bhp at 720rpm. These in turn drive two Niigata Z-peller ZP-31 propulsion units, which give the tug an impressive bollard pull of 58.5 tonnes and a speed of just over 12 knots. The **Svitzer Bristol** has a fire-fighting capability which incorporates a self-protection spray system for the superstructure. The tug was seen at Newport helping out on 25 September 2008. By 2018 she was part of Svitzer's Immingham fleet on Humberside.

(Danny Lynch)

We now move to Cardiff. Just prior to WWII, two members of the German ship and tug owning family Borchard fled to Britain and formed the Fairplay Towage and Shipping Co Ltd, with offices in London and Bristol. At Bristol they formed a subsidiary, the Commonwealth Steam Tug Co Ltd. In 1948 R & J H Rea Ltd acquired a major share in this company, followed in 1954 by the remaining share and one tug. That tug was the *Exegarth* which was completed at Delfzijl by Scheepswerk Delfzijl, Gebrouder Sander V.H. She was delivered to Fairplay, Hamburg, as *Fairplay XIV* in July 1942. She had an overall length of 94 feet, and was powered by a triple expansion engine of 750ihp. The *Exegarth* was one of four tugs used to set up a base across the Bristol Channel at Cardiff in late 1961. This is where she spent her last four years, being sold to John Cashmore Ltd at Newport for scrap in March 1966.

(the late John Wiltshire collection)

At Cardiff and Barry, the existing private tug operators (W J Guy, Edmund Handcock and J Davies) amalgamated to form Bristol Channel Tugs Ltd in 1962. However in July 1963, R & J H Rea Ltd acquired this business, together with five steam tugs. The Great Western Railway (GWR) had also operated tugs at Cardiff and Barry, and upon nationalisation in 1948 was absorbed into the newly-created British Transport Commission. On 1 January 1963, their five steam tugs passed to the British Transport Docks Board (BTDB). In this view we see one of these tugs, *The Earl*, laid up in the Bute East Dock, Cardiff, on 21 April 1963. She was a twin-screw tug, built in 1931 for the GWR by Charles Hill & Sons Ltd at Bristol. In July 1963 the BTDB sold its Cardiff and Barry towage interests to R & J H Rea Ltd. It is unlikely that *The Earl* ever worked again after this photograph was taken, as she was towed to Newport in August 1963 to be broken up at John Cashmore's wharf on the River Usk.

(the late John Wiltshire)

The **Plumgarth** and her sister **Avongarth** were delivered to R & J H Rea's Bristol and Avonmouth fleet in 1960, replacing the steam tugs **Danegarth** and **Corgarth**. The **Plumgarth** was completed by W J Yarwood & Sons Ltd at Northwich on the River Weaver in Cheshire. She was one of the four tugs transferred to Cardiff in late 1961, passing to Cory Ship Towage in 1970. Here she is in Rea colours on 16 March 1968 leading the tanker **Regent Royal** into the main lock at Cardiff.

Although for many years a Cardiff tug, the **Plumgarth** was regularly based at Barry for periods during the late 1960s. In 1979 she moved to the Plymouth fleet based at Torpoint, and was re-united with her sister **Avongarth** once again. She remained at Plymouth until 1985 when she was sold to Greek owners at Heraklion, Crete.

(the late John Wiltshire)

By the late summer of 1964 Rea had sold a number of their recently acquired steam tugs for scrap. They now had eight tugs based at Cardiff and Barry, but only two of these were motor vessels. The decision was made to invest in a small fleet of new motor tugs, and an order was placed with Richards (Shipbuilders) Ltd of Lowestoft to supply a tug with a 15 tonne bollard pull for evaluation. It was delivered in March 1965 as **Lowgarth** and was powered by a 920bhp 7-cylinder Ruston & Hornsby engine. She had a spacious wheelhouse with good all-round visibility, and her propulsion benefitted from a steerable Kort nozzle. The **Lowgarth** passed to Cory Ship Towage in 1970 with the R & J H Rea business. This is how we see her at Cardiff on 29 March 1975, as she approaches the Queen Alexandra lock on a very high spring tide.

(Nigel Jones)

The brief evaluation of **Lowgarth** led to an order for a group of four similar tugs from Richards (Shipbulders) Ltd. They were delivered during 1966, and enabled the last of the steam tugs at Cardiff and Barry to be withdrawn, which sadly included the splendid **Westgarth** of 1954. The first tug to be delivered was **Butegarth** in January 1966. An 8-cylinder Blackstone engine had been chosen for these four tugs. This developed 850bhp, giving a bollard pull of 14 tonnes. Other changes from **Lowgarth** included the use of a small jib in place of traditional lifeboat davits, and also the fitting of slightly deeper windows in the wheelhouse. This shot of **Butegarth** in her original Rea livery was taken on 25 April 1970 standing off the main lock at Cardiff. The **Butegarth** transferred to Newport in 1979, and after her sale in 1989, she eventually settled down with Portuguese owners. As **Lutamar** she was still at work at Lisbon in 2018.

(Nigel Jones)

The **Simson III** was a 100-ton steam-powered floating crane owned by the British Transport Docks Board in South Wales. She had been built in 1925 and was normally based at Cardiff. On 12 June 1977 the crane is being returned to port by the local Cory tugs **Lowgarth** and **Butegarth**. The eagle-eyed will note that both tugs have now been equipped with radar, a feature confined to **Bargarth** for many years at Cardiff and Barry. Work for the **Simson III** steadily declined as trade at Cardiff and Barry became more specialised, and she was eventually broken up for scrap at Cardiff, leaving the South Wales ports without a floating crane.

(the late John Wiltshire)

On the gloomy wet autumn morning of 25 November 1968, the French ocean-going tug *Abeille No. 26* arrived at Cardiff with the Greek cargo ship *Maria M.* in tow. The voyage had started out from Gibraltar, and the *Maria M.* then went into long term lay-up at Cardiff. The *Maria M.* of 2681grt was owned by Biniaris and Veroutis of Piraeus, and was built in Belgium in 1947 as *Gand* for Belgian owners Armament Deppe S.A. The *Abeille No. 26* was completed in 1960 at St Nazaire by Ateliers et Forges de l'Ouest with a gross tonnage of 324 and overall length of 126 feet. She was delivered to Société Provençale de Gestion Maritime (PROGEMAR) and was managed by Les Abeilles International Towage Co. Registered at Le Havre, the *Abeille No. 26* was powered by a 1280bhp Polar type diesel which gave her a speed of 13½ knots. After 22 years' service with PROGEMAR, the *Abeille No. 26* was sold to Société Cherifienne de Remorquage et d'Assistance in 1982. She was renamed *El Majid I* and registered at Casablanca under the Moroccan flag. Her fate after about 2000 is not known.

(the late Des Harris)

The *Cleddia* and *Neylandia* were a pair of Dutch-built motor tugs completed in 1958 by Scheepswerf P de Vries-Lentsch, Alphen a/d Rijn. They were built for Overseas Towage & Salvage Co Ltd's ship towage subsidiary Milford Haven Tug Services Ltd. However they were too small to be of any use at the newly-opened oil terminals at Milford Haven, and were sold to R & J H Rea Ltd in 1961. They were renamed *Falgarth* and *Tregarth* respectively at Bristol, with *Tregarth* soon moving to the new Rea operation at Cardiff until her sale in 1970. The *Falgarth* remained on the English side of the Bristol Channel, and visited Cardiff to help out from time to time. We see her there on 25 May 1971. She was transferred to the new Cory tug base at Plymouth in 1972, and remained there until her sale to Greek owners in 1980. She was initially renamed *Aetos* in 1981, and received many subsequent names. She was laid up at Eleusis in 2017 as *Kapetan Napoleon*, and her subsequent fate is unknown.

(the late John Wiltshire)

During its later years the management of Newport Screw Towing had passed to Powell, Duffryn Ltd. In the summer of 1970 the shares, towing contracts and the four tugs of Newport Screw Towing were sold to Cory Ship Towage Co Ltd, but only *Duncurlew* and *Dunsnipe* were to have a future in South Wales. This view dates from 7 August 1970, and the *Dunsnipe* has just received the Cory funnel colours. Her hull still bears the yellow name and lining of her previous owner. By early August 1970 the complete dock system at Newport was closed for three months to enable major maintenance to be carried out in the main sea lock which dated from 1914. During this period the *Duncurlew* and *Dunsnipe* were based at Cardiff. The *Dunsnipe* became *Gwentgarth* in 1971, and was sold to Greek owners at Piraeus in 1981 being renamed *Adamastos*. It is thought that her working life in Greek waters was brief, and after sustaining damage, she was laid up for many years and broken up by 1992.

(Nigel Jones)

On 20 January 1971 the West German tugs *Fairplay II* and *Fairplay XI* delivered the stricken Cypriot-flag cargo ship *Petros* from Aberdeen to Cardiff. She arrived with a heavy list and laden with a cargo of pit props from Archangel, hence the need for two tugs. For the *Fairplay XI* this was her third visit to Cardiff in less than four years. The catalogue of incidents that had befallen *Petros* between September 1970 and January 1971 is quite astonishing, and is nothing short of a miracle that she ever made it to Cardiff at all. This included a fire on board at Newcastle, failing to take bunkers at Archangel, running out of fuel and running aground near Lerwick, suffering a boiler flashback and being struck by two ships while moored at Aberdeen. The 1240bhp *Fairplay II* of 136 tons gross was essentially a harbour tug and normally based at Hamburg. She was completed in 1959 by Theodor Buschmann Schiffswerft AG, Hamburg, and delivered to Fairplay Schleppdampfschiffs Richard Borchard GmbH, Hamburg. The *Fairplay XI* was completed at Emden in 1963 as *Aro* for Reederei Adolf A Ronnebaum, Emden, passing to Fairplay in 1964. Both tugs remained in the Fairplay fleet until 1990.

(the late John Wiltshire)

The British Transport Docks Board owned the Surrey Commercial docks in London, which closed in December 1970, and some of the redundant quayside cranes were shipped to Cardiff for further use. To avoid dismantling the cranes, they had to be shipped by sea, and this took place in July 1971 and again in April 1973. The German tugs *Argus 5*, *Argus 6*, *Argus 7*, *Argus 8* and *Büffel* were involved, all being operated by Ulrich Harms GmbH & Co, of Hamburg. The *Argus 5*, *Argus 6* and *Argus 7* arrived at Cardiff towing loaded pontoons and a floating crane. The *Argus 7* is seen standing off the lock entrance on 26 April 1973. She was completed in 1970 by Gutehoffnungshütte Sterkrade AG Rheinwerft, Walsum, and was powered by an 8-cylinder Deutz type diesel of 980bhp. The *Argus 7* later passed to Danish owners in 1987 as *Egesund II*. In 1991 she moved to the Mediterranean having been purchased by Impresa Ing. Sparaco Spartaco SpA of Naples who renamed her *Francesco*.

(the late John Wiltshire)

The **Danegarth** was another of the group of four similar tugs from Richards (Shipbulders) Ltd based on the **Lowgarth** design of 1965. The **Danegarth** was completed on 22 April 1966 and delivered to R & J H Rea Ltd at Cardiff. The name **Danegarth** had previously been carried by a steam tug that served with Rea from 1915 until 1960. The new **Danegarth** had a gross tonnage of 161 and an overall length of 95 feet. She had a fixed-pitch propeller that was mounted in a steerable Kort nozzle. Apart from helping out at Barry and occasionally at Avonmouth, she remained based at Cardiff until the arrival of the two new tractor tugs. This view of her dates from 2 August 1975. She then transferred to Newport in 1979 along with **Butegarth**. She was based at Newport until her sale to Greek owners in 1992. By 1993 she was to be found at Heraklion, Crete, and operating as **Linoperamata** for Linoperamata Shipping Company. She was still active as such in 2018.

(Nigel Jones)

This nice study of **Avongarth** was taken on 29 March 1975. She was over at Cardiff to help with two arrivals, one of which was the **Swedish Wasa** on her maiden voyage. The **Avongarth** was the sister ship of the **Plumgarth** (page 26), but remained based at Avonmouth when R & J H Rea set up their tug operation at Cardiff and Barry. In this view, **Avongarth** is in the livery of Cory Ship Towage and transferred to Plymouth in 1979 teaming up with **Plumgarth**. This pair of tugs benefitted from a flying bridge, which was often used by the tug skipper in the warmer weather. When her owner was restyled Cory Towage Ltd in 1985, **Avongarth** remained in the fleet, and was used for coastal towing. In late 1989 she was sold to an owner based at Totnes who renamed her **Tiverton**. This was short-lived as in 1990 she passed to Portuguese owners as **Galito**. By 2000 and still in Portugal, she was with LUTAMAR of Setubal as **San Vicente**, and working in the Lisbon area. She was recycled in 2006.

(the late John Wiltshire)

The United States Army had a large number of motor tugs and the designation LT stood for Large Tug. The **LT-1974** was to design 3006 and was constructed by Higgins Boat Co Inc, New Orleans, in 1953, one of fourteen completed by this yard. She had an overall length of 107 feet and was powered by a 6-cylinder two-stroke Fairbanks-Morse diesel of 1200bhp, which gave her a speed of just over 12 knots. A number of these tugs eventually crossed the Atlantic and the **LT-1973** and **LT-1974** had served in France and the Azores in the 1960s. A small fleet was then based at Hythe on the Solent, and at least two of

them were sent around to Cardiff for dry-docking in the 1970s. On 10 June 1976 the **LT-1974** is moored adjacent to the Commercial Drydock in the Roath Basin; her US outline, apparently based on a WWII, design is unmistakable. At some point **LT-1974** acquired the name **Champagne-Marne** and in 1997 was sent back to the United States, and based at Fort Eustis near Newport News, Virginia. By 2003 she was operating for the U.S. military out of Kuwait in the Arabian Gulf.

(the late John Wiltshire)

In the early 1970s activity at the drydock of Commercial Drydocks Ltd in Cardiff's Roath Basin started to pick up and quite a few tugs received attention there. Between December 1971 and August 1972 seven tugs from Alexandra Towing Co's Swansea-based fleet visited Cardiff to undergo their annual survey. The *Canning* and her two sisters *Wallasey* and *Waterloo* were among these. The *Canning* is bathed in low winter sunshine as she lies afloat in the drydock on 1 December 1971. She was built in 1954 and had a gross tonnage of 200. The *Canning* went on to become the last steam tug operating in the Bristol Channel.

(the late John Wiltshire)

The motor tug *Mumbles* was the newest tug from Swansea to visit the Commercial drydock in this period. She makes quite a contrast to the *Canning* in this view taken on 30 April 1972. She was new in February 1969 and she was a much larger vessel at 291 tons gross and with an overall length of 112 feet. As we can see clearly, *Mumbles* is a single-screw vessel that benefitted from a large steerable Kort nozzle. She was ordered by Alexandra Towing to serve the new tidal harbour at Port Talbot, as well as perform the occasional coastal towing duty.

(Nigel Jones)

The *Anglegarth* was the sister ship of *Dalegarth* (page 10 upper). She was completed in 1960 by Henry Scarr Ltd, Hessle, for service with R & J H Rea Ltd at Milford Haven. In 1970 she passed to Cory Ship Towage Ltd, and soon after was displaced at Milford by the new G-class tugs. The *Anglegarth* was sent to work in Newfoundland, Canada, in October 1970, along with *Dalegarth* and *Thorngarth*. This was until two new tugs arrived for the Point Tupper oil refinery contract. After performing the role of spare tug, *Anglegarth* went on to serve in the Caribbean and Venezuela, until returning to UK waters in 1976, when she was allocated to the Avonmouth fleet. On 9 October 1977 she had come across from Avonmouth to assist with the sailing of the Shell tanker *Amastra* from the Channel drydock. In 1979 *Anglegarth* sailed to Piraeus for a new life as *Leon* with Greek owners Andreas & George Kyrtata. Remarkably, she is thought to be still in service in 2018.

(Andrew Wiltshire)

Delivered in May and June 1979 respectively, the *Holmgarth* and *Hallgarth* are a pair of tractor tugs, the first of this type to enter service in the Bristol Channel. They each featured a pair of forward-mounted Voith Schneider propulsion units. They are seen here moored in the Roath passage at Cardiff on 14 July 1979, looking as smart as the day they were delivered. They joined the Cory Ship Towage fleet based at Cardiff, but were regularly found working at both Barry and Newport. They were completed on the Clyde at the yard of Scott & Sons (Bowling) Ltd who had their yard at Bowling. They were part of an order for four tugs, the other pair to a slightly different design, being destined for use at Grangemouth. Both *Holmgarth* and *Hallgarth* served the Bristol Channel until 2008, and after sale continued to work in British waters.

(the late John Wiltshire)

The **Holmgarth** is seen approaching the lock at Cardiff on 5 April 1980. She was powered by a pair of 6-cylinder Ruston diesels, delivering a total of 2190bhp, and had a bollard pull of 23 tonnes. In 1985 Cory Ship Towage changed their title to Cory Towage Ltd, and with this came a new and more colourful livery. During the 1990s and due to the downturn in shipping at Cardiff and Barry, **Holmgarth** was based at Liverpool for a number of years. In 1998 she sailed to Dublin for a period on charter to the Dublin Port and Docks Board, but eventually returned to the Bristol Channel. She passed to Wijsmuller Marine in early 2000 and subsequently to Svitzer Marine Ltd in October 2001, who had taken over Wijsmuller's UK operations..

(the late John Wiltshire)

On 2 September 1982, **Point James** was a welcome visitor from the Avonmouth and Portbury fleet. She had come across to Cardiff for the evening tide to assist with the docking of the bulk carrier **Finntimber**. As mentioned on page 13, **Point James** and her sister **Point Gilbert** were built for a contract at an oil terminal in eastern Canada which had come to an end by 1980. Both were moved to Avonmouth as they were ideal for use at the new Portbury dock. The **Point James** visited Cardiff on many occasions, but had been transferred to the Belfast fleet by about 1994. Following an engine failure in heavy seas in 1996, she was abandoned and almost became a loss. However **Point James** was rescued and put back into service. Her sale in 1999 to a Caribbean owner was not completed, and she therefore passed with the Cory fleet to Wijsmuller Marine in 2000. In 2002 she was sold and renamed **Saint James** for an Italian owner and registered in Panama. She was sold to a Turkish buyer in 2005, and was eventually recycled at Aliaga in 2009.

(the late John Wiltshire)

After putting in barely two years' service at Newport, the port which she was built to work in, **Dunosprey** remained part of Cory's Belfast fleet for 22 years. However her days in Northern Ireland came to an end in 1992 when she was replaced by the larger **Glengarth** of 1970. The **Dunosprey** was transferred back to South Wales and based at Cardiff and Barry, where she immediately fell out of favour with local tug crews due to the nature of her main engine transmission. To obtain an astern movement, the engine would have to be stopped and reversed, which was considered unacceptable. Here she is at Cardiff on 22 September 1992, but she would soon be moving on. Later that year **Dunosprey** passed to Allan C Bennett & Sons Ltd, Rochester, for use on the Thames and Medway as **Linda Bennett**. After suffering a major engine failure in 1997 she was sold for use as a houseboat and moved to Hoo Marina. She was renamed **Tug Pelican** and received her original Newport Screw Towing funnel colours once again. It is thought she still exists in 2018.

(the late John Wiltshire)

In your author's opinion **Hallgarth** and **Holmgarth** look at their best in the livery of Cory Ship Towage (page 39). The new colours of Cory Towage Ltd introduced in 1985 were based on the lines of the R & J H Rea colour scheme, but the funnel used white in place of silver, and the word Cory in place of a large R. On 19 August 1989 **Hallgarth** was caught making a hasty departure from the Queen's lock at Cardiff. The H-boats, as they were sometimes known, were powerful, compact tugs and their manoeuvrability was really impressive. Their Ruston diesel engines had a distinctive deep note when under load. During the 1990s as the work for her in South Wales declined, the **Hallgarth** was chartered on a number of occasions to provide cover at both Devonport and Portsmouth naval dockyards. Here she would work alongside tugs of the Royal Maritime Auxiliary Service and later Serco Denholm. Eventually **Hallgarth** was sold in 2008 to Falmouth Towage Co Ltd, and began a new life as **St Piran** at this Cornish port.

(Nigel Jones)

This view of **Holmgarth** taken on 5 November 1990 makes an interesting comparison with the view of her just over ten years earlier on page 38. She is now carrying Cory Towage Ltd colours and is seen moored at the Empire Stores wharf in the Queen Alexandra dock. Her deckhouse is now cream which is an improvement to the brown used hitherto. Handrails were later added to the area in front of the wheelhouse of both **Holmgarth** and **Hallgarth** giving a somewhat cluttered look to her superstructure. In 2008 **Holmgarth** was sold to Fowey Harbour Commissioners who renamed her **Morgawr**. She was still at work at this Cornish port in 2018

(the late John Wiltshire)

The **Carew Castle** was a tug with a long and varied history. In this view taken at Cardiff on 20 September 1992, she is performing the role of a survey vessel, hence the rig on her stern. She had been working in Bristol Deep from Walton Bay to the English and Welsh Grounds light float. This survey was in conjunction with the plan to get larger ships up channel to Portbury. The **Carew Castle** is wearing the funnel colours of West Coast Towing and her owner at this time was Haven Maritime Ltd, Pembroke Dock. The **Carew Castle** was completed in December 1959 as **Thorngarth** for Wm Cory & Son Ltd, and managed by R & J H Rea Ltd, Milford Haven. In 1970 she passed to Cory Ship Towage Ltd who soon put her to work in Newfoundland. Cory then transferred her to Cork in 1972 under Irish registry, and she became part of Irish Tugs Ltd (Cory Ship Towage Ltd) in 1979. She was sold to Pounds Marine, Portsmouth, in 1983 suffering from main engine defects. After a long period laid up, in 1990 she passed to Haven Maritime Ltd, who renovated her for further service. She had a number of other subsequent owners and ended her days as **Falmouth Bay** working in Spanish waters and registered in Panama. She was recycled at La Coruña in the summer of 2011.

(Nigel Jones)

West Coast Towing (UK) Ltd purchased the anchor-handling supply tug **King Loua** in 1994 for coastal and ocean towing. While dredging in Cardiff Bay, the dredger **Big Boss** was holed. The **King Loua** towed her to Milford Haven for dry-docking on 31 May 1995, and it is thought that she went to collect **Big Boss** for her return to Cardiff after repair. This view of **King Loua** was taken as she left Cardiff on 30 August 1995. She was eventually sold by West Coast Towing in 1996, and by 1997 was operating in Nigerian waters for Blue River SA, London, and under Panamanian registry. She is believed to be still active in 2018. The **King Loua** was completed in 1972 as **Swordfish** for Feronia International Shipping SA and registered in Djibouti. She was constructed by Chantiers et Ateliers de la Perrière, Lorient, and was a twin-screw vessel of 240grt. She was powered by a pair of Nohab-Polar diesels delivering 2100bhp.

(Nigel Jones)

The second tug to be delivered from the group of four from Richards (Shipbulders) Ltd was *Uskgarth*. She arrived from Lowestoft in March 1966 and took up her duties at Barry. The *Uskgarth* had a gross tonnage of 161 and an overall length of 95 feet. By the time this photograph was taken on 5 July 1991, *Uskgarth* was operating for Cory Towage Ltd, and she was one of the first tugs based in the South East Wales fleet to receive the new Cory Towage livery in 1985. As work at Barry docks tailed off during the mid-1980s, tugs were rarely stationed there, being sent down to the port from Cardiff or Newport, only when required.

(the late John Wiltshire)

The Dutch tug *Tarka* was a Damen Shoalbuster type 2409 that was completed in April 1996. She was constructed by Scheepswerf Damen BV, Bergum, and completed shortly after at their Gorinchem yard. She was delivered to Herman Sr BV (J L van Dodewaard), and registered at Zwijndrecht. She had a gross tonnage of 135 and an overall length of 81 feet. She was powered by two 12-cylinder Caterpillar diesels developing a total of 1358bhp. This gave her a bollard pull of 17½ tonnes, and she was further enhanced by a bow thruster unit.

On 8 September 1997 we see *Tarka* underway in Queen Alexandra dock. At this time she was involved with the construction of the Cardiff Bay barrage, a major civil engineering project. By 2003 *Tarka* had been sent to West Africa to work for German owner Bilfinger Berger AG in Nigeria. In 2004 she was renamed *Berger Explorer* for Julius Berger Nigeria PLC and registered at Lagos. She was still at work in Nigerian waters in 2018 as *Explorer* for Tarkwa Marine Ltd.

(the late John Wiltshire)

The Japanese-built *Westgarth* was the third tug to carry this name and added a welcome bit of variety at Cardiff on the sunny evening of Sunday 17 May 1998. She was built at Yokosuka by Hanazaki Zosensho K. K, and completed in 1983 as *Yashima* for Daito Unyu K. K, Tokyo. She was purchased by Cory Towage Ltd in 1992 following the success with the smaller Japanese-built *Avongarth* (see page 23 lower). She was renamed *Westgarth* and put to work at Avonmouth and Portbury. The *Westgarth* was a typical Japanese Z-peller tug and was powered by a pair of 6-cylinder Niigata diesels developing a total

of 3000bhp. She had a bollard pull of around 40 tonnes and speed of 11 knots. She passed to Wijsmuller Marine Ltd in 2000 and to Svitzer Marine Ltd the following year. The *Westgarth* was initially sold to Cypriot interests in 2016, but was soon resold to M. V. Cargo Ltd (Intresco Ltd, Odessa), and placed under the Liberian flag with no change of name. In May 2018 she was confirmed as working at the port of Yuzhnyy in the Ukraine, still sailing as *Westgarth*.

(Nigel Jones)

The *Forth* is seen at Cardiff on 26 April 2002 in the distinctive colours of Wijsmuller Marine. Her name gives us a clue to her origin. She was one of a pair of Voith Schneider tractor tugs ordered by Cory Ship Towage for service at Grangemouth with Forth Tugs Ltd, her sister being *Carron*. The *Forth* was actually delivered as *Laggan*, and was the last tug completed on the Clyde by Scott & Sons (Bowling) Ltd. These tugs were similar to *Hallgarth* and *Holmgarth*, but the Scottish pair were fitted for fire-fighting from new, and had extra accommodation beneath the wheelhouse. After the sale of an older tug named *Forth* in 1986, the *Laggan* took this name in 1987. In 2000 Forth Tugs Ltd was absorbed into Cory Towage Ltd, which was then taken over by Wijsmuller Marine and subsequently Svitzer Marine Ltd. In 2002 *Forth* was transferred to South East Wales, and in 2003 was renamed *Bargarth*. She worked at Newport, Cardiff and Barry, and was sold in 2009 to Tuskar Shipping Gibraltar Ltd, and managed by Fastnet Shipping Ltd, at Waterford. She was still in service with Fastnet in 2018.

(Nigel Jones)

SMS Towage Ltd can be traced back to 1992 with the formation of Specialist Marine Services. A move into harbour towage on the Humber took place in 1992, and the title SMS Towage came into being. In 2012 Associated British Ports invited SMS Towage to set up a base in South East Wales as Svitzer Marine were cutting back their presence at Newport, Cardiff and Barry. The *Trueman* is an azimuthing stern drive (ASD) tug that was completed in 1987 in Japan by Imamura Shipbuilding Co Ltd, Kure. She was built for Hong Kong Salvage & Towage Co Ltd, Hong Kong, as *Tai Tam* and her sister in the SMS fleet is *Tradesman*, formerly *Waglan*. The *Trueman* has a bollard pull of 35 tonnes, and is powered by two 6-cylinder Niigata diesels, driving a pair of Z-peller propulsion units. In this view *Trueman* is in the Roath Basin at Cardiff in September 2014. She is assisting the Serco Denholm tugs, *SD Independent* and *SD Indulgent* with the berthing of visiting Type 45 destroyer HMS *Duncan*.

(Paul Andow)

Moving west, we come to the port of Barry. This superb shot portrays the motor tugs *Lowgarth* and *Uskgarth* acting as bow tugs on the fully-laden ore carrier *Bamburgh Castle* as she entered Barry on 4 August 1967. The *Bamburgh Castle* was owned by Bamburgh Shipping Co Ltd, Newcastle upon Tyne, and managed by W A Souter & Co Ltd. With a gross tonnage of 11894 and an overall length of 512 feet, she was quite a large vessel for Barry docks. Both tugs are in the colours of R & J H Rea Ltd, which suited them very well. The *Danegarth* had been brought from Cardiff to assist, while the other Barry residents in 1967, *Bargarth* and *Plumgarth*, were most probably on the stern of the ship.

(the late John Wiltshire)

49

The **Bargarth** is seen off Barry, returning to the lock on 1 August 1970. She is looking resplendent in the recently applied colours of Cory Ship Towage, who took over the R & J H Rea business earlier in the year. The **Bargarth** was the final tug of the four delivered from Richards (Shipbulders) Ltd at Lowestoft, and she arrived at Barry in July 1966, to join **Uskgarth**. These tugs and the earlier **Lowgarth** were fitted with a steerable Kort nozzle to improve their bollard pull. The **Bargarth** also had a distinguishing feature as she was the only tug at Cardiff and Barry to boast radar from new. However, by the 1980s this vital navigation aid was standard on all tugs in South East Wales. During the 1970s, the Geest banana ships and the pumice import trade provided regular work for the Barry tugs, but this was also a period when the port was used for the short-term lay up of many ships.

(the late John Wiltshire)

The **Plumgarth** was regularly based at Barry following the departure of the last steam tugs in 1966. However she eventually settled down at Cardiff by 1970, but remained a regular visitor helping out at the port until her transfer to Plymouth in 1979. This view of her acting as a stern tug was taken in April 1971. The **Plumgarth** is now wearing the colours of Cory Ship Towage introduced after the takeover the previous year of R & J H Rea Ltd. In the background on the left is what has become the Atlantic Trading Estate while over the stern of the tug is Sully. The **Plumgarth** was powered by an 870bhp Ruston & Hornsby engine which gave her a bollard pull of 13½ tonnes, but unlike later Rea tugs, she did not benefit from a Kort nozzle. Upon sale to Greek owners in 1985, **Plumgarth** was renamed **Minotavros** for Minos Shipping Company, and had her flying bridge removed and her mast repositioned. She was still in service at Heraklion in 2018.

(Danny Lynch)

The USS *Mosopelea ATF-158* was an Abnaki Class Fleet Ocean Tug constructed for the United States Navy for service in World War II. She was launched at the Charleston yard of Charleston Shipbuilding & Drydock Co on 7 May 1945, and commissioned two months later. A total of 22 Abnaki Class tugs were completed between 1942 and 1945, with some examples later seeing service in the Korean and Vietnam conflicts. They were single-screw vessels with a displacement of 1589 tons. Propulsion was diesel-electric with four General Motors diesels driving four generators geared to a single shaft. In her early days, the USS *Mosopelea ATF-158* would have had a complement of 85 and would have been armed with anti-aircraft guns. She was in Barry on 29 June 1980. The USS *Mosopelea ATF-158* was struck off the US Naval register in 1992 and it is known that she was sunk as a target in October 1999 during a training exercise.

(the late John Wiltshire)

Holyhead Towing's *Afon Goch* was a visitor to Barry on 24 February 1987 to collect a barge. She was built as *Karet* in 1967 by Richards (Shipbuilders) Ltd, Lowestoft, as a terminal tug for NV Curaçaosche Scheepvaart Mij. She was based at Royal Dutch Shell's large oil refinery at Willemstad in the Netherlands Antilles. The *Karet* was a fire-fighting tug of 280grt and was powered by a 16-cylinder English Electric diesel of 2250bhp. From 1974 she was managed by Smit Curaçao Towage NV and later by Shell Tankers BV. In 1983 she returned to the UK having been purchased by Holyhead Towing Co Ltd. She was renamed *Afon Goch* and had a new wheelhouse fitted at Liverpool. With a revised gross tonnage of 232, she was used for coastal towage. The *Afon Goch* was sold in 1991 passing to Maltese interests as *Elena B*. She returned to the UK once again in 1997 joining the newly-established fleet of Portland Towage Ltd as *Sandsfoot Castle*. From 2003 she was *Pioneer* with Murray Tugs, Queenborough, and put out on various charters. By 2012 she was up for sale and was in a sorry state, but by 2016 she had been renovated and was sailing under the Togo flag as *Marie*.

(the late John Wiltshire)

On 12 June 1982, whilst bound from Stanlow to Curaçao, the chemical tanker *Essi Silje* suffered a serious engine room fire in the Atlantic Ocean. Two tugs were sent to assist the *Essi Silje*, and one of these was the Dutch *Gelderland* of 1981. It is believed she acted as the stern steering tug while the *Essi Silje* was towed to Barry by the larger German tug *Baltic*. The *Gelderland* was an early ASD type tug, and one of four similar vessels constructed for IJmuiden-based Bureau Wijsmuller NV. She was powered by two Bolnes diesels developing 2400bhp and driving a pair of Niigata propulsion units giving her a bollard pull of 34 tonnes. The *Gelderland* was placed in service in the Goedkoop fleet at Amsterdam as indicated on her hull in this view of her taken at Barry on 5 July 1982. In 1986 she was sent to Colombia for a charter to Intercor based at Puerto Bolivar. In 1988 she was acquired by CARBOCOL, Puerto Bolivia, and renamed *Ciudad de Riohacha*. She is thought to be still in service in 2018.

(Andrew Wiltshire)

In this view we see the West German tug *Baltic* moored alongside the fire-damaged *Essi Silje* in the No. 2 Dock at Barry also on 5 July 1982. The *Baltic* was owned by Bugsier Reederei und Bergungs AG of Hamburg, and was one of their smaller salvage tugs at 662grt and with an overall length of 167 feet. She was completed in 1969 by F Schichau, Bremerhaven, and was capable of fire-fighting. She was powered by a 12-cylinder Deutz diesel of 3000bhp which gave her a bollard pull of 45 tonnes. Due to a downturn in work, Bugsier placed the *Baltic* into lay-up at Bremerhaven in 1983. She was sold in 1986 to North Atlantic Towage & Salvage Ltd, Valletta, and put back to work as *Atlantic Rescuer* under the Cypriot flag. By 2005 she had been abandoned when anchored off the Namibian coast at Walvis Bay, and was still there in 2011. A sad end to a fine tug.

(the late John Wiltshire)

When **Bargarth** passed to Cory Towage Ltd in 1985 she soon lost her Cory Ship Towage livery and received the colour scheme of her restyled owner. In 1986 **Bargarth** was selected for conversion to a combi-tug which increased her bollard pull from 14 to 17 tonnes. She was sent to the Lowestoft yard of George Prior Engineering Ltd and was fitted with a retractable forward-mounted Aquamaster 420 azimuthing bow-thruster unit. At the same time her aft deck was re-constructed and a towing winch and fairlead were installed. She was back in service during 1987.

By this time **Bargarth** had nominally been transferred to Irish Tugs Ltd, with Cory Towage as her managers. However she continued to work at Cardiff and Barry with occasional visits to Newport. In 1991 she was placed under the Irish flag, with her port of registry changed to Westport, and remained as such until 1998. This view of **Bargarth** was taken at Barry on 28 May 1999. By then she had reverted to British registry and carried the Cory houseflag on her wheelhouse.

(Nigel Jones)

This splendid shot of **Uskgarth** was taken off the breakwaters at Barry on the afternoon of 6 July 1993. The tug is in pristine condition for her 27 years, and highlights the very attractive colour scheme used by Cory Towage from 1985 until their demise in 2000. Also visible in this view are the tug **Christine** which is inbound from the jack-up platform also in the picture. In the distance the lighthouse on Flat Holm Island has been highlighted by the sun, while the larger island Steep Holm lurks behind. In 1995 **Uskgarth** was sold to Bluebird Shipping Ltd, Mauritius, and renamed **Tamar** in 1996 under the Belize flag. By 2002 she was lying derelict at a location in the eastern Mediterranean, and was thought to have been broken up shortly afterwards.

(Nigel Jones)

On 20 July 1989 two tugs from the Clyde Shipping fleet arrived at Barry with some new lock gates which had been fabricated on the Clyde. In this late evening view *Flying Phantom* has just passed through the breakwaters with her tow. The *Flying Phantom* was a large fire-fighting tug of 347grt that was completed at Port Glasgow by Ferguson Bros (Port Glasgow) Ltd in late 1981. She was delivered to Clyde Shipping Co Ltd, Glasgow. Her main engine was a 6-cylinder Ruston diesel of 2820bhp which drove a controllable-pitch propeller in a steerable Kort nozzle. Her bollard pull was increased from 38 to 43 tonnes in 1997 when she was fitted with a 600hp Aquamaster retractable bow-thruster unit. Clyde Shipping had passed to Cory Towage Ltd in 1995, ultimately passing to Svitzer Marine in 2001. The *Flying Phantom* was a tug of misfortune as in December 2000 she ran aground and was hit by her tow before being beached. She was salvaged immediately and eventually returned to service. Tragedy struck near Clydebank in December 2007 when in fog, *Flying Phantom* was overtaken by her tow, girted and rapidly sank. Three of her crew of four were lost. She was later raised and towed away pending an investigation. It was not until 2015 that she was scrapped at Roseneath.

(Bernard McCall)

The other tug to arrive at Barry towing new lock gates was *Flying Spindrift*. She was a newer and quite different type of vessel for Clyde Shipping Co Ltd, Glasgow. The *Flying Spindrift* was a twin unit ASD Z-peller tug with a gross tonnage of 259 and a bollard pull of 40 tonnes. She was completed in 1986 on Humberside by Richard Dunston (Hessle) Ltd. She is seen here in the No.1 dock at Barry on the following day together with *Flying Phantom*. In 1994 she was transferred to associated fleet Lawson-Batey Tugs Ltd and put to work on the River Tyne, passing into Cory Towage ownership in 1995. The *Flying Spindrift* was taken into Wijsmuller Marine ownership in 2000 passing to Svitzer Marine in 2001. She was transferred to the South East Wales fleet by 2007 and to Felixarc Marine in 2009. In 2012 she was sold to FFS-A/S of Farsund in Norway and renamed *FFS Atlas*. She is still hard at work in 2018.

(Andrew Wiltshire)

By the mid-1990s, shipping activity at Cardiff and Barry had reached an all-time low. Consequently only a handful of tugs were required, and these were normally based at Newport. On 10 April 1993 the *Gwentgarth* was acting as stern tug turning the Bahamas-flag reefer *Diamond Reefer* at Barry. The colourful Cory Towage livery suits her particularly well, and her massive funnel is certainly eye-catching. The *Gwentgarth* was a popular tug with crews being of a compact design with an overall length of just 93 feet. She was powered by a 6-cylinder MWM diesel which gave her a useful bollard pull of 22 tonnes. The *Gwentgarth* was transferred to Irish registry in 1990, but remained based in the Bristol Channel until her sale in 1997. She then spent eight years in northern Spain as *Remmar* at the small port of Marin to the north of Vigo.

(Nigel Jones)

This superb portrait of **Hallgarth** was taken as she departed Barry on the afternoon tide of 17 May 1992. She was most probably heading back to Cardiff. When completed back in June 1979, her registered owner was given as Finance for Shipping (R A Napier), with Cory Ship Towage as her manager. From 1985 her manager changed title to Cory Towage Ltd, and the livery changed as shown here. It is thought that during the 1980s both **Hallgarth** and her sister **Holmgarth** were modified so that they could be used as fire-fighting tugs, although no permanent fire-fighting monitors were ever installed

(Nigel Jones)

The British salvage tug *Anglian Lady II* visited Barry on 6 August 1989 to tow away a pipe-laying barge that had been used in the laying of a new outfall near Cold Knap. The *Anglian Lady II* was owned by Klyne Tugs (Lowestoft) Ltd and had an interesting past. She was built by Cochrane & Sons Ltd, Selby, and delivered to United Towing Ltd, Hull, in late 1966 as *Welshman*. In 1974 her owners became Star Offshore Services (Tugs) Ltd, although she continued to be managed by United Towing Ltd. In 1978 she was sold to J P Knight (Rochester) Ltd, Inverness, and renamed *Kinluce* while based at Invergordon for North Sea oilfield related duties. She eventually passed to Klyne Tugs in 1988 as *Anglian Lady II*. She was a twin-screw tug powered by a pair of Ruston diesel engines developing 3250bhp resulting in an approximate bollard pull of 36 tonnes. In 1992 she passed to Spanish owners initially as the *Vikingo* for Remolques del Atlantico Ramay SL and later as the *Kochab* for Puertos y Obras SA, La Coruña. By 2001 she was with owners in the United States under the Panamanian flag, but was laid up out of use at Aransas Pass, Texas, by 2004. She was broken up at Rockport in 2007.

(Andrew Wiltshire)

The **Pisces L** was one of the four Russian-built tugs attached to West Coast Towing Co's new tug base at Newport. The **Pisces L** had previously been the East German tug **Wisent** and based at Rostock. She had been built in 1974 in the USSR by Leningradskiy Petrozavod, Leningrad, and was powered by a pair of 6-cylinder Russkiy diesels of 1200bhp driving a pair of controllable-pitch propellers. Here she is seen assisting in No. 2 Dock at Barry in November 1993, while in the background is the Dow Corning chemical plant. The **Pisces L** did not receive a more appropriate West Coast Towing name and was sold in 1995 to Inversiones Alaria SA for operation by Compañía Sudamericana de Vapores at Valparaiso, Chile, as **Daule**. This was a brief move as in 1996 she was working at Guyaquil in Ecuador. By 2009 her owner was given as Ecuaestibas SA, and she is thought to be still in service in 2018.

(Danny Lynch)

Not only was **Bargarth** the final tug of the four delivered from Richards (Shipbulders) Ltd at Lowestoft back in 1966, but she was the last of the quartet to work in South Wales. The **Butegarth** was sold in 1989 followed by **Danegarth** in 1992 and **Uskgarth** in 1995. The **Bargarth** survived until 2002 which meant she passed to Wijsmuller Marine Ltd in February 2000 and subsequently to Svitzer Marine Ltd on 1 October 2001. She was kept busy up until her sale to Waterford-based Bilberry Shipping & Stevedoring Co Ltd in 2002, whereupon she was to sail under the Irish flag once again. In 2009 she was sold again, this time to Marine Asset Management Ltd, Appledore, and was renamed **Tennaherdhya**. She was managed by Keynvor Morlift Ltd and registered in the Scilly Isles. In late 2017 she passed to TTM Services (UK) Ltd and was renamed **TTMS Viking**. In this view taken on 22 July 2000, **Bargarth** is in the livery of Wijsmuller Marine, which really does look out of place on a tug of her age.

(Nigel Jones)

The **Nobleman** was the former German tug **Rotesand** that began life working on the River Weser at Bremen and Bremerhaven. She was built in 1976 for Unterweser Reederei AG, Bremen. Constructed by Jadewerft at Wilhelmshaven, she was a twin-unit Voith Schneider tractor tug powered by a pair of 8-cylinder Deutz diesels, giving her a bollard pull of 28 tonnes. In 2009 she passed to Survey & Supply (I B Harvey) of Grimsby and had her name shortened to **Tesa**. She was back with Unterweser Reederei AG in 2011 as **Rotesand**.

She was acquired by SMS Towage Ltd, Hull, in early 2012 and renamed **Nobleman**. On 1 March 2012 SMS Towage launched a new tug base in the Bristol Channel with three tugs, the **Trueman**, **Roman** and **Nobleman**. The **Nobleman** is seen here at Barry on 25 July 2012. By 2015 she had returned to Germany and was working out of Emden. Renamed **Friedrich Wessels**, she was operated by Emder Bugsier- und Bergungsgeschäft P W Wessels Wwe. KG.

(Paul Andow)

Our journey westwards brings us now to Port Talbot. The dock at Port Talbot was completed in 1837 and is thought to be the first major dock to be constructed in South Wales. In the 1890s it was linked to the railway network and enlarged. With beach and funfair at Aberavon forming the backdrop, *Formby* makes a fine sight as she heads out into Swansea Bay on 12 June 1969. She was built in 1951 initially for service at Liverpool and was one of three sister ships completed by Cochrane & Sons Ltd at Selby. They were each powered by a 1000ihp triple expansion steam engine built by C D Holmes of Hull. The *Formby* was converted from coal to oil burning in April 1960 and received a shorter funnel. She was transferred from Southampton to Swansea in 1968. Four months after this photograph was taken, *Formby* was joined at Swansea by her sister *Canada*, and both tugs were handed over to Italian owner Fratelli Barretta of Brindisi. They were renamed *Poderoso* and *Strepitoso* respectively.

(the late John Wiltshire)

The construction of large steelworks at Port Talbot in 1902 and Margam in 1916 required large quantities of coal and iron ore. Coal was sourced locally but iron was imported through the port, which witnessed its trade increase dramatically. Some tugs were stationed at Port Talbot while others were sent across from Swansea when required. The *Empire Sybil* was a Hoedic-class Empire tug constructed by Cochrane & Sons Ltd at Selby. She entered service in August 1943 with the Ministry of War Transport and was based on the River Tyne. In 1946 the sale to a Cardiff tug owner fell through and instead she passed to the Mersey Docks and Harbour Board, Liverpool, as *Assistant*. In 1962 she was the last steam tug to be purchased by Alexandra Towing Company, taking the name *Caswell* for a seven year career based at Swansea. Here she is seen leaving Port Talbot before heading out into Swansea Bay. In 1969 *Caswell* was replaced by a motor tug and was towed away to Passage West near Cork for breaking up.

(the late Des Harris)

The Swansea registered motor tug *Margam* is seen underway in the dock system at Port Talbot in March 1969. She was acquired by Alexandra Towing Co Ltd in 1966 and, with an overall length of just 86 feet, was an ideal vessel to work at Port Talbot with its small lock. She was previously the *Caedmon Cross* of Tees Towing Co Ltd (William H Crosthwaite & Son), Middlesbrough. Completed in 1953, she was the forerunner of the similar tugs *Golden Cross* and *Ingleby Cross* (both 1955), which can be found on pages 7 and 18 in this book. The *Margam* was also a product of Scott & Sons (Bowling) Ltd and was powered by a 750bhp Crossley diesel. Having replaced an elderly steam tug, *Margam* put in four useful years' service, pending the opening of the new tidal harbour in 1970. At this point she was sold to Dutch owner Sleepdienst Willem Muller N.V. of Terneuzen and was renamed *Rilland*. In 1971 she was re-engined and a new smaller funnel was fitted, which instantly changed her appearance. Later passing to N.V. Bureau Wijsmuller, she was sold on in 1989 to J Koek of Dordrecht. Soon after on 22 November 1989, she sank in the Bay of Biscay.

(Danny Lynch)

A new tug was launched on 9 February 1960 by Charles Hill & Sons Ltd, Bristol, as speculative build and was unofficially named *Lindsay*. After trials she was eventually sold to Alexandra Towing Co Ltd in August 1960 as *Cambrian* for use at Port Talbot, and registered at Swansea. This view of her dates from 30 January 1970 and clearly illustrates her rather small wheelhouse and funnel. The *Cambrian* had a gross tonnage of 163 and was powered by an 8-cylinder Ruston & Hornsby diesel engine developing 890bhp. Surprisingly after just twelve years' service she was sold in 1972 to Malta Ship Towage Co Ltd and spent the rest of her working life at Valletta. In 1981 she passed to Tug Malta Ltd and her name changed to *Mari*. By 1996 she was out of use and in February 1997 she was towed away to Turkish shipbreakers at Aliaga as *Mar*.

(the late John Wiltshire)

The Dutch tug **Stentor** is seen approaching the lock at Port Talbot at around noon on 26 July 1969, and has in tow a number of barges. They would be used in conjunction with dredging operations for the new tidal harbour works which were now nearing completion. The **Stentor** was owned by Bureau Wijsmuller of IJmuiden and had a near sistership, **Nestor**. The **Stentor** was completed in 1958 by A van Bennekum Machine & Scheepswerf, Sliedrecht, and had a gross tonnage of 192. She was a single-screw tug powered by a pair of 8-cylinder Bolnes diesels which gave her a bollard pull of 16 tonnes. Shortly after her visit to Port Talbot her bridge was modified to incorporate a radio shack which extended aft to her funnel, and spoilt her lines slightly. Wijsmuller sold **Stentor** in 1981 to G. O. R. Enterprises Ltd, who renamed her **G. O. R. Fleet No. 7** under the flag of the Cayman Islands. Just less than three years later she was lost off the Mexican coast after striking a buoy she was attending.

(Danny Lynch)

The Alexandra Towing Company persevered with steam propulsion throughout the 1950s, and a further three new tugs were delivered from Cochrane & Sons Ltd at Selby in 1954. All three were intended for service at Liverpool and carried local Mersey names. The *Wallasey* was the second tug delivered in June 1954 and was also the second vessel in the history of Alexandra Towing to carry this name. The *Wallasey* had a gross tonnage of 200, and was powered by a 950ihp triple expansion engine. She was transferred to Swansea in 1956 and was converted from coal to oil burning in September 1961. This superb view of *Wallasey* was taken on 18 March 1970. Comparing this view to that on page 63, the beach at Aberavon is deserted and the hills in the distance still have a wintry look to them as a storm threatens.

(the late John Wiltshire)

West Coast Towing chartered the powerful twin-screw *Strathfoyle* from the Londonderry Port & Harbour Commissioners during 1997 to help out handling the large bulk carriers at Port Talbot tidal harbour. Here we see her in Swansea Bay on 26 May. Some readers may recognise *Strathfoyle* as the former Red Funnel tug *Clausentum* from Southampton. She was a twin-screw vessel of 366 grt that was completed by Richards (Shipbuilders) Ltd at their Lowestoft yard. She was delivered to her owner the Southampton, Isle of White & South East Royal Mail Steam Packet Co. Ltd (Red Funnel Tugs) in early 1980. She had a bollard pull of 37 tonnes and was fitted for fire-fighting. She left Southampton in 1993 and was retained by her Londonderry owners for nine years. In 2002 she became *Westsund* for Danish owner Svendborg Bugserselskab A/S (Niels Henriksen), and was registered at Svendborg. Used mainly for coastal towing, she was still at work as *Westsund* in 2018.

(Danny Lynch)

When West Coast Towing purchased the former Alexandra Towing tug *Margam* in 1997, she carried on doing what she had done so well for the previous 27 years. That is safely assisting large bulk carriers into and away from the dedicated berth in Port Talbot tidal harbour. She was given the name *Hurricane H.* which had been carried by a smaller tug until 1995. She was powered by a 2190bhp Ruston & Hornsby diesel and also had some fire-fighting capability. This view of *Hurricane H.* was taken on 15 March 1999 as she pushed up to a bulk carrier in the company of *Conor*. After passing to Wijsmuller Marine in May 2001, and subsequently to Svitzer Marine, she was sold in 2007, and in 2018 was sailing as *Voukefalas* for Poseidon Salvage & Towage Maritime Co, Piraeus.

(Danny Lynch)

When opened in 1970, the tidal harbour at Port Talbot was capable of receiving ships of over 100,000 tonnes deadweight, but following a major dredging project in 1996, was then able to accommodate ships of up to180,000 tonnes deadweight. Larger and more powerful tugs were now essential. The *Shireen S* was purchased by West Coast Towing (UK) Ltd in 1997 to work at Port Talbot. She was previously *Kelty* and was acquired from Forth Tugs Ltd, Grangemouth. She was one of the four tugs that were for many years based at the Hound Point terminal, and made redundant when the towing contract passed to another operator. The *Kelty* was constructed by Richards (Shipbuilders) Ltd,

Lowestoft, in 1976 and she and her sister *Almond*, were the two non-firefighting tugs in the quartet. She had a grt of 322 and was a single-screw tug of 2680bhp powered by a 12-cylinder vee-type Ruston diesel. West Coast Towing passed to Wijsmuller Marine Ltd in May 2001 as the tug operator Wijsmuller Port Talbot Ltd. Here we see *Shireen S.* in Wijsmuller livery at Port Talbot harbour. This era was short-lived as Svitzer Marine Ltd took over in 2002. The *Shireen S* was sold in 2005 to Saga Shipping & Trading of Oslo, without a change of name, and by 2007 was under the Panamanian flag. In 2013 she became *W. Power* under Moldovan registry.

(Danny Lynch)

The **Svitzer Lyndhurst** is a large Voith Schneider tractor tug that spent a period based at Swansea. This view dates from 5 February 2010. The **Svitzer Lyndhurst** was completed as **Lyndhurst** during 1996 by McTay Marine Ltd, Bromborough, for service with Howard Smith Towage Ltd at Southampton. She was of a similar design to six tugs completed for service at Immingham between 1990 and 1996. As can be seen in this view she is fitted for fire-fighting and her stern is designed to push up against the side of a vessel. Her main engines are a pair of 6-cylinder Ruston diesels developing 4016bhp and giving her a bollard pull of 43 tonnes. The **Lyndhurst** passed into Adsteam Towage Ltd ownership in 2001 and was renamed **Adsteam Lyndhurst** in 2006, and **Svitzer Lyndhurst** in 2007. In 2018 she was based at Grangemouth.

(Danny Lynch)

Following the Svitzer takeover the existing tugs were gradually sold off and more modern vessels were transferred into the Swansea and Port Talbot fleet. The *Willowgarth* was completed for Cory Towage Ltd, Liverpool, in July 1989. She was equipped for fire-fighting and one of her duties was to serve the Tranmere oil terminal on the Mersey. She was a large tug of 392grt and was constructed by Richards (Shipbuilders) Ltd, Lowestoft. Her propulsion consisted of a pair of Schottel azimuthing units mounted under her stern which gave her a bollard pull of 45 tonnes. Away from the Mersey, *Willowgarth* has worked overseas in Angola in the 1990s, and also spent a period at Belfast. In more recent years she has been based at Swansea and also helps out at Avonmouth and Portbury when required. This view of her taken off Port Talbot clearly shows her open stern, a modification carried out for her work in Angola. In 2018 she is still at work in the Bristol Channel.

(Danny Lynch)

In 2000 the Dover Harbour Board replaced its two 1984-built Voith Schneider tractor tugs *Deft* and *Dextrous* with a pair of powerful stern-drive tugs. At only 16 years old they were a good buy for Howard Smith Towage Ltd, who renamed them *Shorne* and *Cobham* respectively and put them to work in its Gravesend fleet. They were eventually part of the take-over by Adsteam Towage Ltd in 2001, moving on to Svitzer Tugs Ltd in 2007. The same year the pair was transferred to Humber Tugs Ltd, and became *HT Scimitar* and *HT Cutlass* respectively. They were later transferred to the Bristol Channel which is where we see *HT Cutlass* laid off Port Talbot on an overcast 21 January 2010. She was powered by a pair of 6-cylinder Ruston diesels developing 2672bhp and giving her a useful bollard pull of 29 tonnes. After a short spell based in South East Wales, in 2013 *HT Scimitar* and *HT Cutlass* were transferred overseas to Svitzer (Americas) Ltd. They now work in Venezuela.

(Danny Lynch)

The Svitzer fleet serving Port Talbot was regularly changing and in addition tugs were drawn from Avonmouth and even Milford Haven to help out at times. As part of a fleet upgrade Svitzer ordered ten similar tugs from the Lithuanian yard of Baltija Shipbuilding Yard JSC at Klaipeda. They were azimuthing stern-drive (ASD) tugs of around 380gt and with double-skin hulls. The class was deployed around a number of tug bases in northern Europe and included the *Svitzer Marken*, *Svitzer Mull* and *Svitzer Milford*. The latter, completed in 2004, was initially based at Milford Haven. The *Svitzer Milford* is a fire-fighting tug equipped with a self-protection dousing system. Her propulsion consists of two 6-cylinder MAK 6M25 diesels of 4890bhp that drive a pair of Aquamaster propulsion units. The result is a bollard pull of 62 tonnes ahead, while 58½ tonnes can be achieved going astern. The *Svitzer Milford* is seen off Port Talbot on 7 January 2009, with *Flying Spindrift* in the background. In 2018 *Svitzer Milford* is based at Greenock, having also had spells of work on the River Mersey.

(Danny Lynch)

In this early morning photograph, **Dalegarth** is attending to the berthing of a bulk carrier on 11 April 2009 along with the **Yewgarth** and **Westgarth**. She is a stern-drive Z-peller type tug with a bollard pull of 45 tonnes. The **Dalegarth** has an interesting history as she and her sister were some of the first Japanese-built tugs to enter service in a UK fleet. Following the successful operation of the former Japanese tug **Kinross** at Invergordon from 1981, J P Knight acquired the brand new tugs **Yokosuka Maru No. 1** and **Yokosuka Maru No. 2** in 1985. They were brought to the UK and renamed **Kestrel** and **Kenley** respectively.

The **Kenley** was soon put to work on the Medway but **Kestrel** was chartered to Cory Towage Ltd in 1986 and sent to work at Panama. She later moved on to a charter in Mexico and in 1990 was purchased by Cory and renamed **Strongbow**. She returned to work on the Mersey in 1991 and was transferred to the Milford Haven fleet in 1992 as **Dalegarth**. In 2001 she was taken into the Svitzer Marine Ltd fleet, later moving to Swansea. In 2018 she sails as **Europa** in the Black Sea for Romanian owners.

(Danny Lynch)

Our final port is Swansea. The Alexandra Towing Co Ltd established a base at Swansea and Port Talbot in 1924. In 1969 Swansea was still a very busy port and the local tugs also had to serve nearby Port Talbot. Tankers arriving to load refined products such as petroleum and diesel oil continued to provide much work at Swansea for years to come. The BP refinery at nearby Llandarcy directly supplied its output to the loading terminals in Queens Dock. It might well be winter time, but the photographer continues to record shipping movements at Swansea, often in striking lighting conditions. On 28 January 1969 the BP tanker **British Patrol** has just entered the lock. The stern tugs on this occasion are the steam tug **Waterloo** of 1954 and the motor tug **Talbot** of 1961.

(the late John Wiltshire)

The steam tug **Brockenhurst** spent a good portion of her life based at Swansea but had quite an interesting past. She was built by John Cran & Co Leith and delivered to Alexandra Towing Co Ltd, Liverpool, as **Gladstone** in 1913. She had a gross tonnage of 214 and was powered by a compound steam engine built by the shipyard. After less than twelve months in service she passed to the Russian Government along with **Huskisson** of 1912. The **Gladstone** was renamed **Salvage Steamer No. 2**, later changed to **Kersoness** in 1914, and she was put to work in the Black Sea. In May 1918 she was seized by the Germans but taken as a prize by UK forces in November of the same year. In 1923 she passed back to Alexandra Towing Co Ltd and was refitted. She was initially allocated to Southampton as **Brockenhurst**, but later moved back to Liverpool. She was transferred to Swansea in 1939 and remained there until 1964. At this point she was sold for scrap, and is believed to have been broken up at Cardiff by Cox & Danks Ltd. Observant readers will note that her funnel is fitted with a ' spark arrester ' necessary for coal burners when working at oil terminals, with tankers or installations and ships engaged in carriage of explosives.

(the late Des Harris)

The Alexandra Towing Co Ltd purchased two former Ministry of War Transport Empire tugs for service at Southampton. The **Brambles** was acquired in 1950 having worked at Scapa Flow and Harwich. She was a Birch class tug that was completed by Henry Scarr Ltd of Hessle in April 1942 as **Empire Teak**. The **Brambles** had a gross tonnage of 242 and was built as a coal-burning tug. Her triple expansion engine was manufactured by C D Holmes & Co and had an output of 1000ihp. Her boiler was later converted to oil firing and she transferred to Swansea in 1964. Here she is in Kings Dock on 18 June 1968. The **Brambles** was withdrawn from service in 1969, and sold to Northern Slipways Ltd, Dublin, but the sale fell through. She was eventually broken up by T W Ward Ltd at Briton Ferry, during the autumn of 1971.

(the late John Wiltshire)

The **Canning** was the last of the three steam tugs delivered new to Alexandra Towing Co Ltd in 1954 for service at Liverpool. She was completed by Cochrane & Sons Ltd of Selby and handed over in July that year. She was also their third tug to carry this local Merseyside name. The **Canning** had a gross tonnage of 200 and an overall length of 102 feet. Her main steam engine was a triple-expansion unit manufactured by C D Holmes & Co Ltd of Hull which had an output of 825ihp. She had a speed of around 12 knots and unlike her two sisters, **Wallasey** and **Waterloo**, her boiler was oil-fired from new. Having been replaced by a new motor tug at Liverpool, **Canning** was transferred to Swansea in 1965. Here we see her on the afternoon of 1 July 1970, just outside the main lock. She put in ten years' service at Swansea until being retired in 1975, as the last operational steam tug in the Bristol Channel. The **Canning** duly passed to Swansea City Council's Swansea Maritime and Industrial Museum for preservation. In 2018 she is part of the National Waterfront Museum at Swansea.

(the late John Wiltshire)

The *Flying Kestrel* was the first of the two former Empire tugs acquired by Alexandra Towing Co Ltd for service at Southampton. She too was a Birch class tug that had been completed in 1943 by Henry Scarr Ltd as *Empire Mascot*. She had an overall length of 113 feet and was built as an oil-fired vessel. She had a similar power plant to *Brambles* and this gave her a speed of 11½ knots. In 1946 the Ministry of War Transport sold her to Metal Industries Ltd of Glasgow who renamed her *Metinda IV* in 1947. She passed to Alexandra Towing in 1948 and was renamed *Flying Kestrel* the following year, the fourth Alexandra tug to carry this name. She was transferred to Swansea in 1965 to replace older steam tugs, and put in about four years' service there. Here she is alongside in Swansea on 6 June 1968. In early 1969 *Flying Kestrel* was declared surplus with the arrival of two newer steam tugs from Liverpool. She was sold to shipbreaker Haulbowline Industries Ltd of Passage West near Cork and towed away by the new Swansea tug *Mumbles*.

(the late John Wiltshire)

The *Frans* was a small Dutch single-screw tug that was photographed at Swansea on 3 September 1971. She may have been involved with the construction of the new West Pier. She was completed in 1951 as the *Borggraaf* for 1951 A. V. Mij Uitvoering Openbare Werken of Sliedrecht near Rotterdam. She was constructed by Scheepswerf J Bijlholt, Foxhol, with a gross tonnage of 49 and an overall length of 69 feet. When built she had an MWM diesel of 330bhp, but this was replaced in 1964 with a larger Caterpillar diesel which gave her a bollard pull of just over 6 tonnes. She passed to Sleepdienst Adriaan Kooren NV, Rotterdam in 1964 and was renamed *Frans*. She was still owned by Kooren when on 11 October 1977, she sank off the Dutch coast.

(the late John Wiltshire)

The year 1972 witnessed the departure of a further two steam tugs from Swansea leaving just three in action at the port. The *Waterloo* was sold to Società Rimorchiatori Napoletani early that year, and departed for a new life at the busy Italian port of Naples on 14 February. She was prepared at Swansea and repainted into the livery of her new owner as *Dritto*. Like *Canning* (page 77), the *Waterloo* had been built by Cochrane & Sons Ltd, Selby, but was allocated to the Swansea fleet from new. She was not converted from coal to oil burning until October 1962. This was carried out at Ellesmere Port on the Manchester Ship Canal, after which *Waterloo* spent a short period working on the Mersey, before returning to Swansea. As *Dritto* she worked at Naples for sixteen years prior to being sent to local shipbreakers. She had been broken up by the summer of 1989.

(the late Des Harris)

The Canadian Navy built three large ocean-going tugs in 1955/56 that were known as the Saint class. Two vessels were **St Anthony** and **St Charles** completed in 1955 and 1956 respectively by Saint John Dry Dock. The third tug was **St John** launched on 14 May 1956 by George. T Davie & Sons Ltd, Lauzon. All three were originally operated as Royal Canadian Navy tugs but were later transferred to the Canadian Naval Auxiliary fleet with civilian crews. The **St John** had pennant number ATA 535 and was based in Halifax. With a gross tonnage of 597, her engine was a two-stroke 12-cylinder Canadian Fairbanks Morse diesel of 1950bhp. She had a controllable-pitch propeller and a speed of 14 knots. The **St John** was sold many years prior to her two sisters. In 1972 she passed to European Navigation Co (Eckhardt & Co), of Hamburg. They renamed her **Dolphin X** under the Panamanian flag and put her to work towing redundant ships to a Spanish shipbreaker in Santander. Here she is arriving at Swansea on 10 March 1972 to tow the tanker **British Splendour** to Santander for breaking up. On 28 November 1980 **Dolphin X** sank while towing a barge off the coast of Newfoundland.

(the late John Wiltshire)

As mentioned on page 36, the **Mumbles** was a new tug delivered to the Swansea fleet in 1969 for use at the new tidal harbour being constructed at Port Talbot. She was quite an imposing tug with a raised fo'c'sle and a large wheelhouse and funnel to match. The **Mumbles** was completed at Hessle by Richard Dunston (Hessle) Ltd and was registered at Swansea. Her gross tonnage was 291grt and she had an overall length of 112 feet. The **Mumbles** was powered by a 9-cylinder Ruston & Hornsby engine of 2190bhp and she had a speed of 12 knots. This view of her was taken as she towed the Panamanian tanker **Dona Myrto** out of Swansea on 17 October 1969. The **Mumbles** was included in the take-over of Alexandra Towing Co Ltd by Howard Smith Towage Ltd in 1993, and continued to work at Swansea until 1998. At this point Howard Smith Towage Ltd closed down their tug base at the port due to competition from West Coast Towing. The **Mumbles** was then sold to T P Towage Co Ltd. for service at Gibraltar, and placed under Gibraltar registry. In 2009 she was sold to Portuguese owner LUTAMAR at Setubal and commenced work in the Lisbon area as **Guardiao**.

(the late John Wiltshire)

The name **Alexandra** had first appeared on an Alexandra Towing tug as far back as 1888. The only motor tug in the fleet to bear this name was delivered in 1963 for service in the Liverpool fleet. She had been completed by W J Yarwood & Sons Ltd, Northwich, and was a sistership of **Herculaneum** delivered in 1962. The **Alexandra** was powered by an 8-cylinder Alpha diesel of 960bhp and had a speed of 11½ knots. She featured a controllable-pitch propeller and had a bollard pull of 18 tonnes. The **Alexandra** moved to Swansea from Liverpool in 1965. She is seen here underway heading into Queens Dock from Kings Dock, on 25 July 1969. She passed to Howard Smith Towage Ltd in 1993 and was sold in 1997 to General Port Services Ltd, Rochester, without a change of name. By 2011 she was out of service and was broken up at Erith, Kent in 2015.

(the late John Wiltshire)

The *Waterloo* is seen approaching the lock at Swansea on 8 June 1968 after completing a job sailing the BP tanker *British Gull*. The *Waterloo* was launched by Cochrane & Sons Ltd on the 24 October 1953 at Selby, and handed over to Alexandra Towing on 27 April 1954. She was the first of three similar tugs, the second being *Wallasey* which was launched a month later. The *Waterloo* had an overall length of 102 feet and a breadth of 25 feet. She was powered by a triple-expansion steam engine assembled by C D Holmes of Hull, which gave her an indicated horse power of 825, and a speed of 12 knots. From 1965 until 1972 all three sisters, the *Waterloo*, *Wallasey* and *Canning* were based at Swansea and were regularly to be found working at Port Talbot.

(the late John Wiltshire)

On 7 June 1973 the former Victory ship USNS *Kingsport* of 1944 visited Swansea to load a cargo. She was assisted into port by the steam tug *North Buoy* with the help of the motor tug *Gower* on the stern. In this view we see *Gower* heading out into Swansea Bay to meet the elderly military cargo ship. In 1961 Alexandra Towing received two new motor tugs, both of which featured for the first time a controllable-pitch propeller. They were completed on the River Weaver by W J Yarwood & Sons Ltd, Northwich, as *Gower* and *Talbot* and delivered to their owner in July and October 1961 respectively. They both saw initial service on the Mersey before heading to South Wales. These tugs had an overall length of 95 feet and were powered by an 8-cylinder Crossley diesel that developed 865bhp. Their propulsion was enhanced by a Kort nozzle and they had a speed of 11 knots. The *Gower* continued to serve Swansea and Port Talbot until 1985, when she was sold to Greek owner Panagiotis Koutalidis at Piraeus. She eventually sailed for Greece in 1986 as *Kostas*. She later became *Faethon* and had a number of subsequent Greek owners. By 2010 she was being stripped for spare parts at Volos.

(the late John Wiltshire)

Although not the last steam tug to be built at a British shipyard, the **North Wall** was the last example to be built for a customer in the British Isles. She was launched on 8 April 1959 at the yard of Scott & Sons (Bowling) Ltd on the River Clyde at Bowling. She was completed in June and delivered to Alexandra Towing Co Ltd, and followed her sister **North Buoy** into service at Liverpool. They were generally very similar to the five "North" boats that entered service in the years 1956/57, and which included **North Rock** and **North End**. These in turn were slightly larger versions of the three tugs constructed in 1954, (described earlier). The **North Wall** had an overall length of 104 feet and was powered by a 1050ihp triple-expansion steam engine built by C D Holmes & Co. The **North Wall** was transferred to Swansea in 1969, and is seen at work on 4 September that year. In 1973 she was sold to Fratelli Barretta, Brindisi, and renamed **Maestoso** under the Italian flag. After a respectable period of service at Brindisi she was broken up in late 1988.

(the late John Wiltshire)

In November 1970, the second of the two tugs ordered for use at the new Port Talbot tidal harbour was delivered. She too was built on the River Humber by Richard Dunston (Hessle) Ltd and was named **Margam**. She was of similar dimensions to **Mumbles** of 1969, but had a much less pronounced fo'c'sle. Here she is leaving Swansea on 15 July 1971. During her career at Swansea and Port Talbot **Margam** undertook some coastal towing, and was also part of the Howard Smith takeover in 1993. In 1997 she passed to West Coast Towing (UK) Ltd as **Hurricane H.** and continued to work at Port Talbot as we saw on page 68. She then passed to Wijsmuller Marine Ltd in May 2001 and later to Svitzer Marine Ltd. She finally left the Bristol Channel in 2007 when she passed to Marman UK Ltd as **Hurricane**. Later that year she was working in Greek waters.

(the late John Wiltshire)

This superb shot of **North Buoy** was taken on 28 November 1969, with the old West Pier in the background. The **North Buoy** had been transferred to Swansea in 1969 together with her sister **North Wall**, and along with the new motor tug **Mumbles** they had replaced the older steam tugs **Caswell**, **Flying Kestrel** and **Formby**. The **North Buoy** was also from Scott & Sons' small shipyard and had been launched on 11 September 1958, being completed by early 1959. She was built with an oil-fired boiler and was reputed to have a bollard pull of 13 tonnes and a speed of 11 knots. The steam tug was rapidly becoming an outdated and uneconomical type of vessel by the early 1970s. Those built in the 1950s still had quite a bit of life left in them and soon attracted overseas buyers, with several Italian fleets keen to purchase them. The **North Buoy** followed her sister **North Wall** to Brindisi in 1973 becoming **Coraggioso** for Fratelli Barretta. She too was scrapped at Brindisi in 1988.

(the late John Wiltshire)

The *Waterloo* of 1977 was the third tug for Alexandra Towing Co Ltd to carry this name. She was the second of a pair of powerful but rather top-heavy looking tugs to be constructed by Richard Dunston (Hessle) Ltd. She was a single-screw tug powered by a pair of Ruston diesels with a combined output of 3520bhp. This gave her a very impressive bollard pull of 54 tonnes. Her sister, *Wellington*, remained at Liverpool but *Waterloo* was transferred to Swansea and Port Talbot by May 1978. This view of her at Swansea was taken on 15 May 1979. The following month she was moved to the London fleet based at Gravesend and was sent out to Algeria in 1980 with *Wellington* to undertake a charter at the port of Arzew. Both tugs were unpopular in the Alexandra fleet and were prematurely sold in 1984 to the Ports & Shipping Organisation (Government of Iran). The *Waterloo* was renamed *Ghorban* and was initially based at Bandar Bushehr. It is thought that at least one of this pair was damaged in the Iran-Iraq conflict, but may have been returned to service at some point.

(Nigel Jones)

The *Rana* was completed by Cochrane & Sons Ltd at Selby and delivered to Gaselee & Son Ltd, London, in 1951. She had a gross tonnage of 98 and her main engine was a 750bhp British Polar two-stroke. She was completed with a tall funnel resembling that of a steam tug, but had this replaced by a smaller funnel after passing to Ship Towage (London) Ltd in 1965. After briefly operating at Felixstowe in 1974, and upon passing to Alexandra Towing Co Ltd in 1975, *Rana* was transferred to Swansea. This is where we see her on 27 July 1976. As a Thames river and dock tug she was not designed for open water working, quite why she was sent to Swansea is unknown. The *Rana* was not really suitable for operating in the swell of Swansea Bay in poor weather, let alone crossing to Port Talbot. She was sold to Humphrey & Grey (Lighterage) Ltd, London, in 1978 as *Redriff*, and became *Rana* once again in 1984 upon purchase by Alan C Bennett & Sons Ltd. She later became a houseboat at Hoo Marina in Kent.

(the late John Wiltshire)

The *Fabians Bay* was another former London tug that had put in good service on the Thames for eighteen years, but in 1984 was surplus to requirements. She was completed in 1966 as *Sun III* for W H J Alexander Ltd, London, a product of James Pollock Sons & Co's yard at Faversham in Kent. She was powered by a 6-cylinder Mirrlees diesel of 1340bhp, which gave her a speed of 12 knots. The *Sun III* passed to London Tugs Ltd in 1969 which was absorbed into Alexandra Towing Co (London) Ltd in 1975. Upon transfer to Swansea she was given the local historic name *Fabians Bay*, after a tidal basin that existed on the site now occupied by the Prince of Wales Dock. This view of *Fabians Bay* was taken on 15 March 1988 as she is about to enter the lock from Kings Dock. In 1992 she was sold, along with her sister *Sun II*, to Greek owners at Chalkis. Both remain active in 2018.

(the late John Wiltshire)

The *Sauria* was an attractive-looking tug that was completed in 1968 for service at Felixstowe with Gaselee & Son (Felixtowe) Ltd. She was built by Richard Dunston (Hessle) Ltd and had a gross tonnage of 165 and an overall length of 101 feet. The *Sauria* was a single-screw tug with some fire-fighting capability and was powered by a 1360bhp Ruston & Hornsby diesel. In 1975 Gaselee was taken over by Alexandra Towing Co (Felixtowe) Ltd and the container port at Felixstowe continued to expand. Container ships were getting larger and by the mid-1980s

Sauria was normally the spare tug. In 1987 she was transferred to Swansea for a brief spell and is noted here on 17 April that year. Later in 1987 she was sold to Greek owners as *Triton*, and by 1988 was operating for S Karapiperis, Piraeus, as *Karapiperis VI*. In April 1991 she was the victim of a terrorist attack, and was blown up and sunk at Perama. She was later raised and scrapped nearby.

(the late John Wiltshire)

In 1994 West Coast Towing (UK) Ltd obtained the towing contract for Port Talbot tidal harbour and set up a tug base at Swansea. For this they needed some large powerful tugs and purchased two twin-screw vessels from South Africa. The **C M Hoffe** and **F H Boltman** dated from 1977 and 1979 respectively and were based at the Richards Bay coal terminal north east of Durban. They were delivered new to the South African Government (Railways & Harbour Administration). Their main engines were a pair of 16-cylinder Mirrlees-Blackstone diesels with a combined output of 6522bhp. These drove controllable-pitch propellers which resulted in a bollard pull of 52 tonnes and a speed of 13 knots. With West Coast Towing they became **Ryan** and **Faris** respectively. This view of **Faris** as she leaves Swansea dates from 25 October 1997. After periods with Wijsmuller Marine Ltd and subsequently Svitzer Marine Ltd, she was sold in 2005 to Al Jazeera Shipping of Bahrain for use on a tug/barge contract in the Arabian Gulf. She was renamed **Atlas**, and in 2018 was thought to be laid up.

(Nigel Jones)

Following the delivery of *Margam* in 1970, Alexandra Towing ordered a further four similar tugs from Richard Dunston (Hessle) Ltd. They were deployed at Liverpool and eliminated the last steam tugs from service at the port. They were delivered in order as *Alfred*, *Crosby*, *Albert* and *Victoria* during 1972 and had a gross tonnage of 272. At 2400bhp they were slightly more powerful than *Margam* and had a bollard pull of 40 tonnes. Gradually they moved away from Liverpool with *Victoria* being the first to make a move to Swansea in 1973. By the 1980s *Alfred* was working out of Felixstowe, but moved to Swansea in 1992, and passed into Howard Smith Towage ownership the following year. This is how we see her on the hazy morning of 10 August 1997. In 1999 she was sold to West African owners and became *Defiant* for Togo Oil & Marine. She flew the Togo flag and was last heard of in 2006.

(Nigel Jones)

In 1994 Howard Smith Towage transferred the two former Port of London Authority (PLA) tractor tugs **Burma** and **Dhulia** to Swansea. Here they took the traditional Alexandra Towing names **Langland** and **Caswell** respectively. This shot of the **Langland** dates from 5 July 1997 and clearly shows her unusual layout. The PLA placed four of these single-unit Voith Schneider tugs in service in 1965/66 all with names beginning in Pla. The **Langland** was completed as **Plasma** in 1965 by Richard Dunston (Hessle) Ltd with an overall length of 87ft. She was powered by a 16-cylinder Lister-Blackstone diesel of 1600bhp and had a bollard pull of 16 tonnes. She became **Burma** for Alexandra Towing Co Ltd in 1991 and was based at Gravesend. In 1998 she transferred to Howard Smith (Humber) Ltd, Grimsby, becoming **Lady Joan**.

(Nigel Jones)

The **Egerton** was also a Voith Schneider tractor tug but was of French origin and dated from 1969. She was completed by Ziegler Frères, Dunkerque, as **Subtil** for Société de Remorquage et de Sauvetage du Nord, Dunkerque. Her main engine was a Crepelle diesel of 1430bhp and her bollard pull was quoted as 18 tonnes. In 1990 **Subtil** passed to Union des Remorqueurs de l'Ocean, Bordeaux, and was acquired by Alexandra Towing Co Ltd in 1991 and renamed **Egerton**. It was probably more than a coincidence that Alexandra already had her sistership in their fleet. She was **Sun Swale** which was completed as **Clairvoyant** in 1968 and acquired in 1981. The **Sun Swale** was based in the Gibraltar fleet by 1990. The **Egerton** passed to Howard Smith Towage Ltd in 1993 and transferred to Swansea by 1997. Here she is in Swansea Bay on the morning of 10 August 1997. When Howard Smith Towage Ltd closed its Swansea base in 1998, **Egerton** moved to the Medway passing into Adsteam (UK) Ltd ownership in 2001. Adsteam sold her in 2002 to T P Towage Co Ltd, Gibraltar, where she joined her sister **Sun Swale** and also the former Swansea tug **Mumbles** of 1969.

(Nigel Jones)

The German ASD escort tug **Bugsier 9** was in Swansea on 24 October 2009 for repairs to a fouled propulsion unit. She was a relatively new vessel at this time having been delivered to Bugsier Reederei und Bergungs AG, Hamburg on 10 April that year. She had actually been launched as **Sanmar Eskort 80-2** in December 2008 for the account Sanmar Denizcilik Makina ve Ticaret Lid Sti, Istanbul. She was a RAL 3200-design tug from the associated shipyard of Gemsan Gemi ve Gemi Isl. San. ve Tic. AS, Tuzla, and her sister ship was **Bugsier 10**. This was a very successful design of tug and by 2009; over 70 examples were in service around the world. The **Bugsier 9** has a gross tonnage of 485 and an overall length of 105 feet. She has two Schottel propulsion units mounted under her stern, and was powered by a pair of 8-cylinder Wärtsilä diesels with a combined output of 6528bhp. Her bollard pull ahead is just over 84 tonnes. She is still in service with Bugsier in 2018.

(Danny Lynch)

Another of the relatively new Russian-built tugs acquired by West Coast Towing in 1994 was **Imakon 1**. She was a fire-fighting tug completed in 1992 by AO Gorokhovetskiy Sudostroitelnyy Zavod, Gorokhovets and designed to operate in ice. She had two 8-cylinder Pervomaysk diesels developing 1604bhp and driving a pair of controllable-pitch propellers. West Coast renamed her **E. L. Preston** and she initially worked at Newport. She moved to Swansea when operations at Newport ceased on 5 January 2001. The ship handling operations of West Coast Towing passed to Wijsmuller Marine (UK) Ltd on 10 May 2001, which in turn passed to Svitzer Marine Ltd on 1 October 2001. In February 2002 it was decided to give **E. L. Preston** a Cory-style name and she became **Butegarth**. Here she is looking very smart as she sails from Swansea. However just over a year later she was sold to Euro Baltic Shipping Services, Tallinn, and renamed **Vega I** under the Estonian flag. By 2004 she was under Russian registry as **Poseydon** for Anship LLC, Temryuk.

(Danny Lynch)

The **Battleaxe** was completed as *Lyrie* in 1978 for operation by Shetland Towage Co Ltd. She and her two sisters, **Stanechakker** and **Swaabie**, were constructed by Hall, Russell & Co Ltd, Aberdeen, for use at the Sullom Voe oil terminal in the Shetland Islands. They were large fire-fighting salvage tugs with a grt of 392 and an overall length of 125 feet. They had a bollard pull of 54 tonnes. In 1996 *Lyrie* and **Swaabie** were replaced by newer tugs and passed to Cory Towage Ltd, who renamed them **Elsie** and **Evelynn** for use on a two-year contract at Puerto Armuelles, Panama. The **Evelynn** was then sold and **Elsie** retuned to the UK and was renamed **Battleaxe** for use on coastal towing. She passed to Wijsmuller Marine Ltd in 2000 and was used at Port Talbot from 2001 as seen in this view, passing to Svitzer Marine Ltd in 2002. The **Battleaxe** was transferred to Svitzer Africa (Pty) Ltd in 2007 and sold to Craignish Ltd, British Virgin Islands, in 2010. She was last heard of working in Nigeria, and in 2018 was under the flag of St Vincent and the Grenadines still sailing as **Battleaxe**. *(Danny Lynch)*

The **Ryan** is the second of the two tugs initially described on page 89. She was launched at Durban on 3 July 1977 by Dorman Long VanderBijl Corp Ltd (DORBYL) as **C. M. Hoffe**. She had a gross tonnage of 528 and was powered by a pair of Mirrlees-Blackstone diesels which gave her a speed of 13 knots. After receiving the name **Ryan**, West Coast Towing collected her and her sister **Faris** from Richards Bay on 30 January 1994. They sailed both tugs to the UK, taking bunkers at Cape Town on 3 February and Las Palmas on 21 February. Upon arrival at Newport on 3 March they had each covered 6882 nautical miles. The **Ryan** and **Faris** were regarded as good sea vessels, and ideal for handling large bulk carriers at Port Talbot in the poor sea conditions of Swansea Bay in winter time. This view of **Ryan**, taken on a fine day, depicts her in the livery of Svitzer Marine. She remained in these colours, based at Swansea until her sale in 2005 to Al Jazeera Shipping Co as **Hercules** under the flag of Bahrain.

(Danny Lynch)

In 1980/81 Rea Towing ordered a pair of azimuthing stern-drive tugs from McTay Marine Ltd, Bromborough, for a contract at Chevron's Malongo terminal at Cabinda in Angola. The tugs were named *Eldergarth* and *Rowangarth*. A second similar pair was ordered by Cory Ship Towage Ltd in 1984, but these were slightly larger and more powerful. The first to be delivered was *Oakgarth* which went to Cabinda to replace *Rowangarth*. The *Yewgarth* followed and she was sent to Puerto Bolivar, Colombia, on a joint contract with Wijsmuller. After a further deployment, this time to the Middle East, she eventually returned to Liverpool. The *Yewgarth* was completed in March 1985 and was actually leased, being managed by Cory. Unlike the first pair *Yewgarth* was fitted with Ruston diesel engines which drove a pair of Z-peller propulsion units and delivered a bollard pull of around 50 tonnes. By late 2001 she was with Svitzer Marine Ltd and later moved to Swansea for use at Port Talbot harbour. This view of her was taken in Swansea Bay on 6 September 2005. The *Yewgarth* was sold in 2012 to Black Sea Services Srl, and now works at the port of Mangalia in Romania as *BSV Irlanda*.

(Nigel Jones)

In this view we see the Japanese-built Z-drive tug *Warrior III* in Swansea Bay on 8 July 2009, and bound for dry dock at Milford Haven. The *Warrior III* began life as *Hayakuni Maru* in June 1975 when she was delivered to Nissho Kisen K.K. for service at Tokyo. She is a good example of an early Z-peller ASD tug and has a grt of 199. She was built by Kanagawa Zosen, Kobe, and is powered by a pair of 6-cylinder Niigata diesel engines delivering 2600bhp. Interestingly for a Japanese-built Z-drive tug, she uses a funnel for her exhaust whereas most examples have underwater exhaust discharge in their stern. In 1990 *Hayakuni Maru* passed to Portuguese owner Rebonave as *Montenovo* and in 1993 to Celtic Tugs Ltd, Cobh, as *Celtic Warrior*. She passed to Cory Towage Ltd in 1996 as *Warrior* under Irish registry this name changing to *Warrior III* in 1997 when she came under UK registry. She was based on the Clyde at Greenock passing to Wijsmuller Marine Ltd in 2000. Under Svitzer ownership *Warrior III* spent a period based in the Bristol Channel until her sale to Greek owners in 2013. She passed to the Spanopoulos Group as *Christos XXV*, and was towed away from Avonmouth to Piraeus by the Greek tug *Pantodynamos*.

(Danny Lynch)